INTELLIGENT MOTIVATION, INC.

GoalsBook

Embracing Personal Responsibility

in an Age of Entitlement

Biagio William Sciacca

North American Business Press, Inc

Atlanta, Georgia
Seattle, Washington
South Florida
Toronto, Canada

GoalsBook
ISBN: 9780985394929
© 2012 All Rights Reserved.

Along with trade books and textbooks for various business disciplines, North American Business Press also publishes a variety of academic-peer reviewed journals.

Library of Congress Control Number: 2012952446

Library of Congress
Cataloging in Publication Division
101 Independence Ave., SE
Washington, DC 20540-4320
Printed in theUnited States of America
First Edition

Table of Contents

Table of Contents

This, my first book, is dedicated to the memory of Venerable Father Solanus Casey OFM, who said that, "God's plans are always for the best, always wonderful. But most especially for the patient and humble who trust in Him, are His plans infinitely holy and sublime." The miracles attributed to this holy man, who died the year I was born, are numerous and profound. He is a true testament to the healing power of God, however you define God!

Hey Father Solanus, I know you told me to dedicate this book to my mother out of respect. I asked her the other day, and she said that she would spank me if I didn't give you this honor. Now, look Father, I'm fifty-four years old at the time of this writing; that's too old to be spanked! Hey, you and I go back a lot of years. You were always there for me and I have tried to be there for you. Assist the people reading this book to get as much out of it as they can. Some of the readers may not believe in you, but that's okay, because I know that you believe in them!

www.solanuscasey.org

Acknowledgment

There are so many people to acknowledge in the writing of a book, that the acknowledgment can become a whole book in and of itself!

Let me begin by acknowledging Paul J. Meyer and my friends at LMI. You have spent 20 years doing your best to shape me into a polished professional. I bet within the next 20 years, it may work! My special thanks to Sam Maitz who never gave up.

I would also like to acknowledge the administration, staff, and faculty of Penn State University. You have taught me patience, clarity in thinking, and knowing when I should shut up! (A very tough lesson.)

Jackie, my fiancée was invaluable, in guidance, support, lucidity and total uncompromising belief.

My children Billy and Salvatore, you taught me more that all my university training.

And, all of my thousands of students over the past 30 years, both in academia and professional training; because of you I can think on my feet, communicate fiercely, laugh at myself and be at peace. You are the reason for this book. Never stop believing in yourself!

(You really do need to read this!)

A beginning note . . . You will see the protagonist (the hero) of this book is writing in a specific calendar system. The brand name of that calendar system is called a My-Tyme. Of all the systems I have used throughout the past thirty years, I have found the My-Tyme to be the best. The reason? It tracks both business AND personal obligations; not to mention that it is one of the best organizational systems I have ever found for setting and tracking goals. Information about the My-Tyme is available in the back of the book.

A second beginning note . . . Don't be suspect as to the dedication page! I am Roman Catholic and I believe in my faith, but this IS NOT a religious book—not even close!

This book took six months to write; however, it took thirty years to glean the material necessary to allow it to come to fruition. That's okay; hey, how old would I now be if I *didn't* collect that information?

I am going to do something very uncharacteristic of me. Normally, I like people to discover the value of an idea for themselves, but, this is your lucky day! I am actually going to give you the moral of the story, right here—in the introduction! What's more interesting is that I have not mentioned once the moral in the bowels of the book. Rather, I would hope that the moral residue of each chapter, once combined into a uniform thought pattern, would point you to the true meaning.

One thing that really got me upset about *Think and Grow Rich* was that Napoleon Hill said he would uncover the meaning and it would become self-apparent. When I read that book thirty-odd years ago, I was so hell bent on finding the meaning that I lost the content. I am not going to do that to you. If you want to be shrouded in mystery and suspense, read a Stephen King book. I am just going to tell you.

All right, all right, I can hear you now, "Hey Sciacca, stop telling us that you are going to tell us and tell us already!" Sheesh, here it is—the real meaning of this little work that you are now holding is: Personal Responsibility! That's it, two words: "personal" and "responsibility." But, dear reader, those two words are so very important and so far-reaching in terms of your level of personal success that I don't want to take a chance on the message being lost by subtle context.

Hey, guess what? Emerson was right. Self-reliance rules! You can't pay another person to go to the gym for you, and you can't pay another person to read this book and apply it for you. That is your job.

The concepts that lay herein have earned me a great deal of money throughout the years; but the money, in retrospect, is meaningless. What this material has taught me is intellectual pursuit, a heightened degree of communication and personal freedom to do and explore whatever I want to do and explore! There is a direct correlation between self-discipline and freedom. It really is cause and effect. If you do what you are supposed to do, when you are supposed to do it, you are then free to do what you want to do, when you want to do it! Goal-setting is that process of self-discipline that allows you to truly be free. And, the end result is a true love of life!

Make no mistake, dear reader, I love life. I hope I have conveyed that concept in my humble work. I hope further that I can assist you in moving your life forward with the simple process of setting and achieving goals.

I will say this, in terms of what you have purchased and are now reading: I have tested this material with countless students, colleagues, and clients. The overwhelming response has been positive beyond my wildest expectations.

My hope is that you find it to be the same—lively, exciting, alive with feeling, passion, drama, and the possibilities of being able to accomplish whatever you want to accomplish. If so, thank God, for He is the ultimate author of this material; if not, blame me because I did not convey the message properly.

Why is it that the ocean of life waits for all of us

to come and to get our fill? Yet, some people go to the ocean with a thimble and say, "Well, that's all I'm worth."

And some go with a bucket and say,

"I guess that's enough for me."

And others build a fusion reactor right on the shore

and consume vast amounts of water,

generate great wealth for themselves

and everyone they come into contact with

and, yet, the level of the ocean didn't drop at all!

Life is willing to give us whatever we ask;

the problem exists in the fact

that we simply don't ask for enough.

Interesting, even though we may ask and

take a great deal from life,

it still has an infinite amount to give to others.

It is the well that never dries up,

the tree that is always in bloom.

I would hope that everyone who reads this is looking for more out of life. Maybe it is money, maybe it is happiness, perhaps it is just greater peace of mind, or to spend more time in activities that you, the reader, think is of great importance! Whatever! Want more? Then read on . . .

The young man looked out from the side window of his white Camaro. There was an accident on the road ahead of him. He had hoped that no one was injured too badly. As he drove past the accident, he saw that it was a fender-bender and the owners of the two vehicles were yelling at each other, arms flailing. He smirked to himself and thought they could not be injured too badly if they were bickering with each other with such vehemence. He wondered why both parties simply could not thank God and be happy for not being injured.

As he thought about this, he realized that the traffic was moving again and he was happy. The young man was very punctual and did not want to be late for what he considered one of the most important meetings of his life.

As he pulled into the parking lot of the downtown campus that housed the corporation where he worked, he wondered why the CEO of the corporation wanted to meet with him. As he entered into the commodious vestibule of the corporation headquarters, his mind was still on that important question when Felix, the security guard, welcomed him with his usual, "Good morning!" The young man, normally responding with a bright-eyed good morning, mumbled an incoherent, "Hello."

While in the elevator, which was travelling to the top floor, the executive suite, the young man's mind wandered to his childhood. He was always such a determined young man. He thought back to when he played Little League, how he bugged his dad to play catch with him for hours on Saturday and Sunday afternoon. When his father was worn out, the young man would simply throw the ball into the air and play catch with himself. He thought about the hours of practicing free throws when he was selected for the basketball team in high school. He thought about cause and effect. He remembered being honored for never missing a foul shot. He remembered his time as a crossing guard in the sixth grade and the offices he held throughout junior high school and high school. He remembered his days as president of his college class and the clubs he had been in.

The young man smiled at himself because he knew that he was a go-getter. He knew that he was a real hustler when it came to getting what he wanted. As the elevator came to a smooth, quiet stop, he knew it was that exact attribute of his behavior that was going to get him fired this very day; and not just fired by his boss, but by the CEO of this multibillion-dollar, multinational corporation!

As he entered the outer office of the CEO's sanctum, he was greeted by a pleasant, mature, and very professional woman who was the CEO's personal assistant. She looked up at the young man and smiled. She said that the CEO was expecting him but he would need a few minutes to finish his current business and that the young man should have a seat.

Sitting on the rather expensive feeling leather sofa located next to the door he had entered, the young man picked up a copy of *CEO Q Magazine*. On the cover of the magazine was the very man he was about to see. This man, this CEO, went from extremely humble beginnings to commanding one of the largest, most powerful, and most profitable corporations in the world! The young man read the article with marveling interest and with both admiration and envy. He hoped that someday he would be able to rise to that rank of success and power in the business world. It seemed doubtful at this point since the young man was sure that his termination was imminent.

As he finished the article, he thought that many of the skills the CEO had been lauded for, he himself had, of course to a minor degree due to his relatively young age and lack of experience. After all, he had only graduated from the university several years ago, and he was only halfway through his MBA program. He had years to develop his skills. His fiancé, a graduate of the same high school and university, and an employee of the corporation herself, told the young man on many occasions that he has all the makings of an executive. All he needed to do was work hard, keep his eye on the ball, stay enthusiastic, and stop asking so many questions.

That was the young man's biggest problem—he asked too many questions. He never accepted an answer at face value. He would dig, and dig until he was satisfied with the answer. His supervisor, a man with very little motivational flare or enthusiastic energy to move outside of his comfort zone, told many people in the corporation that the young man was never going to make it. The supervisor said that he (the young man) refused to take direction; everything was an issue—a problem! "Questions, questions, questions," said the young man's supervisor, "All he does is ask questions. This kid is either the most defiant person I ever met, or the stupidest!"

Actually, the young man had an insatiable curiosity. He wanted to know more about everything. So, he asked questions. He wasn't mean-spirited. He wasn't vindictive. He just wanted to know!

His mental process never accepted an answer at its face value; he wanted to know more! He felt driven to dig deeper and to get the kernel of truth that would allow him ultimate satisfaction with regard to the issue at hand.

But, he was sure that many employees looked at him as being strange, rather daft—the kind of employee who started off with a huge bang, but because of a personality quirk, faded quickly and ended up in a safe, nondescript position somewhere in the bowels of the corporation and was only seen at a Christmas party! He thought of lightning at night, how it can make the whole landscape light up like day, but only for a second. Then, afterward, everything seemed darker! He didn't want to be that kind of person.

The CEO's assistant excused herself as she spoke to the young man again. Apparently, she had said something, but the young man, deep in thought, did not hear her. He hoped she didn't think he was being rude; he truly was in heavy contemplation. The CEO's assistant said that it wouldn't be much longer. The young man's appointment with the CEO was for nine and it was nine now. The assistant said that the CEO prided himself on always keeping his promises and commitments, and that included being on time for meetings.

The young man marveled at this. Perhaps the CEO was on the phone right now with a company in China, structuring a multimillion-dollar deal, or maybe he was on a conference call with his executive vice-presidents. Maybe he was talking to the governor of the state (the CEO and the governor were personal friends), or maybe he was talking to the president of the United States, whom he knew personally. He was a business consultant to the president! And, he was going to stop whatever he was doing to speak to the young man. The young man thought with a mental smirk, that the CEO was going to terminate whatever he was doing so he could terminate the young man's employment!

As he shifted restlessly on the velvety leather, he thought about how he used to drive his little league coach crazy with questions about his stance and posture, how to hold the bat, the ball the glove, whatever. Once, during a particularly long practice, on an extremely hot, humid day, the coach actually told the young man, then a boy of twelve, to "Shut the hell up, keep your eye on the ball, and focus!" The young man saw the reddened face of his coach and knew he was frustrating him, but the young man was not sure why. Now, moments before his certain, impending separation from the job that would have secured his future, he knew his "coach" was frustrated with his questions!

As the young man looked up to the wall at the framed pictures of the CEO with other business luminaries, his thought process was interrupted by the CEO's administrative assistant telling the young man that the CEO was ready to see him. She asked if he would like some coffee or another type of beverage. The young man said no at first, then reconsidered, and asked for a glass of water, thinking that if the CEO was to ream him out prior to firing him, he could at least explain himself. Having a nice, moist throat may facilitate that process.

As the woman lead him into the CEO's office, the young man was immediately struck with several sensory impressions simultaneously. One was the brilliant sunlight that entered the office, not only from the windows but from the sections of ceiling that were actually glass. Another was the size of the office. He knew that CEOs had large offices, but the commodiousness of this left the young man's mouth agape.

At the far end of the office was a large desk of sorts. The young man thought it was a desk, yet it had no drawers. Behind the desk was a credenza with one drawer in the middle. (The young man's immediate impression was to ask a question, which he voiced only to himself, "Where do you keep your files?) Flanking the procession area to the desk, on the left was a round ornate table with a silver tea service upon it, and to the right a settee area with a leather sofa and two large, overstuffed chairs, each facing a deep, dark colored coffee table. The floor was a rich hardwood with several thick and beautifully decorated area rugs. The walls, a color darker than the floor but lighter than the tables and desk, were solid wood panels. The next thing the young man noticed was a tall, well-built man in his late sixties or early seventies, with striking grey hair containing several jet black streaks. His face set in a professional yet, friendly grin and was in one of the most beautifully tailored, navy blue pinstriped suits the young man had ever seen.

The young man must have looked laughable to the CEO. As the CEO approached him, the young man stood there, not moving, as if a bear or another wild animal was approaching him. He knew that he should stay perfectly still and perhaps the menace would walk right by him!

The sun reflected from the CEO's impressive, squared face sporting the kind of tan that could only be had with a trip to a tropical area. And, as the CEO reached the young man, hand extended, he said, in a professional but reassuring voice, "Good morning. Please, have a seat." And the CEO swept his left arm semicircularly to the settee behind him.

The young man said thank you and walked quickly to the proffered area sitting in the middle of the couch, bolt upright, with his hands folded in his lap. As the young man thought about how dry his throat was, the CEO's administrative assistant came into the office holding a tray with a bottle of water and a cup of freshly brewed coffee.

She handed the bottle of water to the young man, who forgot to say thank you. He took it, opened it, and chugged several gulps. She offered the coffee to the still standing CEO, who responded with a confident, "Thank you, Mary. Would you be so kind as to hold my calls for the next hour?"

"Certainly sir," came the crisp, clean response.

The CEO waited a few moments for Mary to close the door, and then sat on the large chair to the young man's left. He took a sip of his coffee, made a low sound of, "Ahh," signifying his content with the beverage, looked at the young man, smiled, and said, "Well, I'll bet you're wondering why I asked you here this morning."

The young man, sounding comically like an untalented impressionist doing Daffy Duck, said, "W-w-welll, yeah, er, y-y-yes s-sir."

The CEO laughed a booming, good-natured laugh. He reached over, patted the young man's knee, and said to him, "Don't be nervous. I can understand why you are. I was in the same position you are in many, many years ago, and I was nervous too. But, I am telling you: *don't be!"*

The "don't be," came out with such impassionate assertion that the CEO actually compelled the young man's nervousness to dissipate.

As the sun shone off the CEO's stark white shirt and deeply ingrained red and navy paisley tie, he crossed his legs, sat back and the CEO, too, folded his hands on his lap. His posture was regal, but friendly. The young man felt calm and assured, but there was no doubt who was on the higher level of the food chain. He thought that this must be the way a king in ages past would have received a subject he had summoned—for no purposeful intimidation, but no deep level of congeniality or familiarity either. It was what we would today call professional.

"I understand you have been questioning many of the policies and procedures we have in place here at the corporation. Would you mind telling me about that?"

The young man squeezed the bottle of water prior to speaking and a great dollop of it spilled directly unto his crotch, giving the young man a look of not being able to control his bladder. As he jumped up to avoid anymore spillage, he dropped the bottle on the coffee table, spilling the remainder of the contents over another copy of the magazine that the young man was reading prior; thus soaking the face of the CEO, on the cover.

The CEO laughed again, this time the booming laugh turned into a deep, bursting belly laugh, and through tears in his eyes he said, "My wife told me that I was all wet! Have you been talking to her?"

The young man, beet red, and mouth open, was trying to say he was sorry, but was drowned out by the CEO, still laughing and in a professional, yet slightly louder voice called for Mary.

It seemed that he didn't even get her name out and she was there, assessed the situation quickly, disappeared for a moment, and then reappeared with a thick towel to remove the water from the table. She had a second towel that she handed to the young man also. In a very short period of time, she was finished with her task. She looked at the young man, smiling though speaking to the CEO, and said, "Take it easy on the new employees, will you?" The CEO laughed again, and Mary winked at the young man and left.

"Okay," said the CEO. "Let's try this again. Would you please tell me about your questioning of our policies and procedures? If you have some ideas for improving our operations, I am all ears!"

The young man was relaxed now. All of his adrenalin dissipated making him very tranquil. He spoke, "I'm not looking to make any changes—I am only trying to understand." The young man smiled and continued, "I want to know more! All my life I've been like this. I want to be successful at everything I do. With sports and school it was somewhat easy, but trying to understand this corporation— Wow! This is one complicated machine."

The CEO smiled hearing this distinction. When young people go through school and sports, it is difficult for most of them since it is the first time that they are experiencing it. Most schooling and sports do not change much over time, but the dynamics of a multinational, multi-billion-dollar corporation, change every day.

"So," the young man continued, "I am looking to be successful here at work and I guess I just needed more information than I was being given, so I asked questions. But, well, maybe, I guess, I might have asked too many! Sorry."

"Don't be sorry," said the CEO, "You really can't ask too many questions. At least not until you understand whatever you are looking for. Of course, any strength overused becomes a weakness; but that's not why I called you here."

"May I ask why you did?"

"You may, and it's a fair question. I am always on the lookout for new and exciting talent. I am wondering if that might be you."

"Me? You mean I am *not* going to get fired?"

The CEO looked at the young man with disappointment. His tone was flat and unemotional when he said, "I let the people who work for me do those unpleasant tasks. Me? I'm on the other side of the field. I don't fire the worst—I hire, promote, and retain the best.

"When I hear about bright young people, I talk with them personally. I see if they have what it takes to fill the role for this type of undertaking. You mentioned something a minute ago; you said that you always want to be successful."

"Well, yes sir. Doesn't everyone?"

The CEO smirked and said, "You would be surprised at the number of people I meet who *do not* want to be successful. Tell me, what does that word, "success," mean to you?"

The young man, with a contemplative look on his face, thought hard for a moment and said to the CEO, "Well, I guess that success is different for everyone."

"Absolutely," said the CEO. "Success has to be personal. It would have no meaning otherwise. Oh sure, we can have moments of 'collective successes' such as a group or team moving forward on a notion or goal, but ultimately success boils down to what it means to you. Here is the rub: do you remember from your college days, when you entered a class for the first day—what did the professor do?"

"Well, he introduced himself."

"Then what?"

"Ah, he, went over the syllabus."

"Okay," the CEO said with a kind laugh, "After all the administrative stuff is over and the professor gave you the name of the course to make sure you were in the right place, when he started the lecture, what was one of the first things the professor lectured on?"

The young man drew in a breath, thought for a moment, then said, with a look of enlightenment, "He gave a definition of the topic you are going to be studying."

"Exactly," exclaimed the CEO. "Now, why do you think the professor does that?"

"I guess so that you can put the rest of the course in context. You know, so that when you get stuck later on in the course, you can go back to the definition and put the new material in perspective."

"Yes. Yes!" said the CEO. "That is exactly it!" Now take that information and apply it to what we are talking about now—success."

The young man, with a bit of hesitation, said, "I would say we need a definition of success that is genera—a definition that fits everyone, so you can put later successes into perspective."

The CEO smiled with affirmation and slowly nodded with admiring approval. He said, "Let me see if I can make this a bit clearer. What can you tell me about Warren Buffet?"

"Well," the young man said with a contemplative pause, "He is a multi-billionaire. He donates his time to kids and sings songs. He donates a great deal of money to charitable causes and gets other billionaires involved."

"Would you say that he is a success?"

"My God, yes!" exclaimed the young man. "He's like a rock star!"

The CEO smiled at this seeming incongruous comparison—a rock star and a dyed-in-the wool-capitalist. "Yes, I can see what you mean, he is definitely successful. Now, tell me this: what do you know about Mother Theresa?"

With furrowed eyebrows and a questioning look, the young man said, "I think she was called the Angel of Calcutta. She had no money of her own because she took a vow of poverty. Ah, she started a religious order. And she took care of poor and sick and old people who had no one else to take care of them."

"Ahem, you do know a lot about her. Would you say that Mother Theresa was a success?"

"Oh yes, everyone loved her when she was alive and I think a lot of people pray to her now that she is dead. I think that the Roman Catholic Church is trying to make her a saint." The young man noticed that on the windowsill was a framed picture of the CEO shaking Mother Theresa's hand.

"So," said the CEO, "You said that Warren Buffet is successful and you also said that Mother Theresa is successful. Correct?"

The young man hesitantly nodded. He thought that he was being set up for something, but, he just didn't know what.

"Do you think that they were successful in the same way?"

"Well," the young man said with a slight tone of irritation at the question that could only have one answer, "Of course not." The CEO noticed that sense of tension, almost annoyance in the young man's tone and thought, with a sense of irony and humor, that perhaps he liked to ask questions, not answer them. The CEO mused on this thought for a moment and then continued.

"Can you see why we need to develop a definition of success that would fit both Warren Buffet and Mother Theresa, since they are both very, very different people, and behave very differently, yet are both are very, very successful?"

"Yes," said the young man, I can see why a definition would ground us to that point—to keep things in perspective."

Nodding again the CEO reached into his pocket and pulled out a small piece of paper while saying to the young man, "Exactly! We need to come up with a definition of success general enough to include everyone who is successful. Do you think that you are up to the challenge of discovering the information?"

"Hell yeah!" said the young man with a timber of excitement. "Er, excuse me sir. I mean, yes sir, I would love to look further into this process!"

Once more the CEO gave a great belly laugh and said, "Give this gentleman a call. He is intelligent, high energy, and funny as hell, er, heck."

This time both of them laughed.

The CEO handed the small piece of paper he had taken out of his pocket to the young man. It was a business card. The name and title on the card read

Marvin Huffberg,

Attorney, Principal

With a look of seriousness, the CEO told the young man, "Success is serious business, but the study of it and its implementation should be enjoyable. One step at a time, let's try to figure out what the definition is that fits Warren Buffett & Mother Theresa, then we can figure out how to put it into place. This man, Marv, will give you some ideas. Listen to what he has to say and then do what he suggests. Give him a call; I think he will see you tomorrow morning."

"Tomorrow is Saturday." the young man said.

The CEO smiled and said, "Don't worry, he'll be there."

With that statement, the CEO stood up. This was obviously a dismissal and the young man understood immediately. He thanked the CEO while shaking his hand. He could not believe that he thought he was going to be fired! Instead, now, he understood that his behavior was not only permissible, but also appreciated and encouraged. He would get his answers and find out what it means to become a success.

The young man turned around to give a last thank you to the CEO who was standing behind the chair where he had been seated, arms folded, head cocked, and smiling. The smile showed lines on his face, but they did not show age, they showed wisdom. The young man felt at ease and comfortable, as though he was going to learn something —something grand, something profound. He smiled back.

The young man left the CEO's office. Mary, smiling at the young man, said, "I hope you enjoyed your time with him. He is truly an amazing man. Listen to what he has to say. He knows . . ."

The young man smiled back, thanked her, and nodded his affirmation. He then pressed the button to the elevator and rode it to his floor.

As he sat at the desk in his cubicle, he wrote in his My-Tyme:

Success must be defined.

The definition must work for everyone.

Any strength overused becomes a weakness.

He added:

(Do all successful people work on Saturday?)

Chapter One

Progressive—It Ends at the Beginning

It was a bright, warm Saturday morning in the city where the law firm was located. Actually, the firm was on the other side of town from the corporation. The young man had called Attorney Huffburg yesterday morning, directly after making his notes in his My-Tyme and after his very uplifting and informative meeting with the CEO. He expected to call the law firm's main number and be redirected several times to someone's voice mail who would give Attorney Huffburg the message to call. Hopefully he would be able to call and set up a meeting tomorrow morning as the CEO suggested. To the young man's surprise, the number on the card got him directly to the attorney's administrative assistant. After giving his name, he was again surprised that within seconds of being placed on hold, a gruff, yet friendly voice came on the other end of the phone, "Hello, Marv Huffburg here."

"I, ah, I was a-asked to contact you sir, ah, Mr., ah, Attorney, Huffburg."

"Yes, yes, I know all about that. Call me Marv, all of my friends do, and to the best of my knowledge, so do all of my enemies . . ."

The booming laughter that emanated from the young man's receiver was deafening. "When you really get to know me, you can call me the Jewish Cowboy!" Again, booming laughter.

The gruff voice continued, "Tomorrow morning, 8:00 AM sharp. Don't be late, it's the Sabbath and I have a few loose ends to tie up, then, I don't work! Do you know where my office is located?"

"Yes, I . . ."

1

"Good, see you then . . . and black!"

"Ah, okay. What do you mean 'black?'"

"Black. I take my coffee black. What did you think—that you weren't going have to pay for this meeting?" Booming laughter again. "And make it an extra large! Don't go getting cheap on me before we even meet, I have enough clients like that!" Booming laughter again. "See you tomorrow morning at 8:00 AM, did I mention 8:00 AM sharp?"

"Yes sir."

"Good. And it's Marv, see you then." And, there was silence as the phone was hung up.

As the young man got out of his car holding four extra large black coffees in one hand and his My-Tyme in the other, he started to laugh a bit to himself at the conversation that occurred yesterday. He thought that this guy must be a real character. He must be very smart because he does a great deal of work for the corporation and for the CEO personally.

The building the young man stood in front of was enormous. As he entered the lobby, he saw the regal splendor of the facility. He thought that this must make clients feel very at ease—knowing that because this law firm has made millions of dollars for itself, it had to have made hundreds of millions for its clients. Eclipsed only by the commodiousness of the atrium of the corporation, the young man walked toward the security guard at the far end.

The security guard, a young man with blond hair and blue eyes, who looked like he had spent more of his time at the gym than in his high school classes, looked at the young man and said, "Here for Mr. Huffburg?"

"Ah, yes, I am."

"Elevators are behind me; take any one of them to the top floor. I'll let him know you're on your way."

"Thanks."

"No problem," said the guard as he picked up the phone, turned his back on the young man, and punched in a few numbers.

As the elevator door opened, he heard wafting through the closing elevator door, "Yes, Mr. Huffburg. He is on the way up now."

Rising smoothly and stopping at the top floor, as the elevator door glided open, the young man was greeted with a reception area that rivaled the CEO's—bright, almost intense sunlight, and a grinning, five-foot, five-inch, middle-aged, portly man in Levi jeans and a dark blue tee shirt. On the tee shirt, in bright, white letters was written: The Jewish Cowboy. The man moved very quickly for his girth and as he approached the young man, he extended his hand and said, "Hello young man, my name is Marv Huffburg."

"Hello Mr. Huffburg," The young man said as he balanced the coffees upon his My-Tyme that he had placed horizontally on his left forearm while extending his right.

Booming: "I thought I told you to call me Marv."

Sheepish: "Yes sir, I forgot."

Booming: " 'Sir' is *not* 'Marv.' "

Sheepish: "Oh, yes sir. Uh, I mean Marv."

"Good. Now that we got the formalities out of the way, give me a coffee, come into my office, and let's chat for an hour or so."

The attorney's office was large, airy, and sunlit. All of his furnishings were a traditional motif, with pastels accenting the royal blues and regal reds. The thick carpeting had several additional area rugs over it that gave the office a look of compartmentalization. Some areas were for business, and some areas are for socializing. The attorney took the young man over to what was definitely an area for socializing.

Two love seats in deep brown leather faced each other and were flanked by small, ornate coffee tables containing decorative lamps and various knickknacks.

As the attorney sat in one of the seats, he motioned with his right hand, waving like a magician might do over a black top hat with a white bunny magically appearing. While in the process of his seeming legerdemain, the attorney said to him guffly, "Sit."

As the young man got comfortable, the attorney grabbed a coffee, almost ripping it from the cardboard tray, tore off the lid, and placed the lid on one of the coffee tables. He took a sip, almost a full-fledged slurp from the paper cup, smacked his lips, and made an approving "Ahhh" sound. He placed the cup haphazardly next to one of the ornate knickknacks, spilling some coffee on the white and gold ceramic cherub. He looked at his slight mess with dismay and said, "Damn, if my wife were here she would give me hell, but, fortunately, she is not here, and if you try to give me hell, I'll throw you out! (Booming laughter.)

"Well, young man, I understand that you have made a royal pain in the ass out of yourself!" (Booming laughter.) "Always asking questions. Never accepting the answer given to you. Digging deeper and deeper. Is that true?"

"Yes. But, I don't do it to be mean-spirited. I am only looking for more, or maybe I should say truer information."

The attorney looked at the young man. Actually, he appraised him by gazing at him from head to foot and back up again. The young man felt the power of the attorney's intensity and knew he would never want to be cross-examined by him. The attorney pursed his lips and made direct eye contact with the young man. The young man didn't think he was meant to purposely feel uncomfortable, but he was. The attorney knew that he was analyzing the young man with too great a degree of intensity. He broke eye contact and took another huge gulp of coffee followed by another approving smacking sound.

"So," Mr. Huffburg said, "Let's talk about success. Hum, how do we begin this process of defining a word that is so difficult to define? It's somewhat like trying to grab Jell-o. The harder you squeeze, the less you have!" (Booming laughter.) "Let me ask you something young man, did you ever go on vacation with your parents?

"Oh yes, my brother and sister and I went on vacation almost every year, mostly to the beach but sometimes to the mountains."

"Hum" said Huffburg. "Then, let me ask you something else, when did the vacation begin?"

The young man wasn't sure about the question. Most of the time they left on Friday night or Saturday morning, then drove to their destination. Normally, it took a few hours, actually more like five or six hours, to get to where they wanted to go, then, they stayed until the following Friday or Saturday. After thinking about the question for a while, he said to Huffburg, "Well, either Friday or Saturday."

The attorney chuckled and said, "Let me see if I can clarify the question a little more. Did the vacation start when you got to the destination?"

The young man frowned in deep thought and remembered the time planning the vacation, the brochures, the stops along the way to see some of the sights and grab a quick bite to eat. As his frown changed to a smile of remembrance, he said, "No, the vacation started long before we arrived at our destination. It included the planning, the talking and laughing, and the singing in the car on the way."

With a smile on his face the attorney asked further, "And when did the vacation end?"

Understanding the line of questioning now, the young man responded, "In some cases, our vacations didn't end—even today we still talk about this time or that time."

"Ha, yes, yes!" said Huffburg. "Would you agree that it is not just the destination, that the journey is just as important?"

"Well, I guess so. If we all of a sudden got to the vacation spot we would have missed much of the fun!"

"You got it, young man! You have heard that success is a journey, not a destination. Let me take that further and tell you this: success is a process, it is not an event. Just as you don't 'all of a sudden' get to your vacation spot, you don't 'all of a sudden' become successful. As a matter of fact, you don't all of a sudden become *anything*!"

"I'm not sure I understand that."

"Well," said Huffburg, sounding somewhat impatient, yet understanding the young man's confusion at the same time, "I'm divorced! I was married to my first wife for eighteen years. When do you think that the divorce happened? Let me give you a hint, it didn't happen at year eighteen of the marriage, it happened at about year fifteen! But, you see, young man, there is no such thing as 'all of sudden.' It took three years for the end result of what we both knew was inevitable."

"I think I am beginning to understand what you mean by process and not an event."

"Yes," said Huffburg, There is no such thing as 'all of a sudden.' Let me go further. Tell me, do you like to eat chicken wings?"

Perplexed at the relevance of the question, the young man said, "Well, sure I do. But I don't eat them very often."

"Really, why not?"

"Well, they're really not that good for you."

"Oh?" Exclaimed Huffburg, "You think not? Are you saying that the American Heart Association is saying that a diet rich in saturated fat is not life sustaining?" Booming laughter.

Quiet laughter: "Well, kind of!"

"You're right, and think about why. The fat from those damn wings goes right into your arteries and hardens them up. Then *Bang!* Heart Attack! But remember, there is no such thing as all of a sudden. You don't get a heart attack when you eat one wing, do you? Oh no! It takes eating a bucket of wings, every Saturday night and a dozen wings a few other nights a week for twenty years before you build up enough plaque in your circulatory system for that to happen!

"Let me give you an example: Let's say that you and your fiancée are going to a bar tonight to have a few drinks, relax, and tell her about this intelligent well-built lawyer that you met today! (Booming laughter). And, you notice a guy at the bar ordering a few dozen wings. The wings come out of the kitchen. The guy grabs one, picks it up, the grease is dripping off his elbow. (Booming laughter) He takes a bite, stands up, grabs his chest, and falls over dead!

"You ask the bartender what happened. He says that it's those damn chicken wings. The fat from that wing went right to his aorta, clogged it up, and killed him, and that was the first wing that guy ever ate! Now, think about this: if we knew that one wing would do that to us, would we eat it? Of course not! But, it's not one wing that does that—it's many wings over many years. That's why we keep eating those tasty little cholesterol bombs! (Somewhat booming laughter.) Because, there is no such thing as all of a sudden! If there were such a thing as all of a sudden, at least in this example, we wouldn't behave that way!"

The young man, looking intently at the portly attorney, wondering how he knew that he was engaged, and understood, in an instant an important concept: Success occurs a day, a moment at a time."

Huffburg continued, "We call that part of success *progressive*. Success occurs moment by moment."

The young man smiled. Not only did he understand, he used the same basic wording as this wise, experienced man did!

Huffburg said, "Here is the beauty of success being progressive. We become successful, not when we achieve a goal, but when we define the goal, and modify our behavior so that we can attain it! Success happens at the beginning of the process of goal-setting, not at the end of it."

The attorney was intent, firm, fixed, and focused. Let me repeat that slowly and listen carefully: <u>We become successful, not when we achieve a goal, but when we define the goal and modify our behavior so that we can attain it!</u> Success happens at the beginning of the process of goal-setting, not at the end of it. Do you understand what I said?"

With wide-eyed amazement, the young man looked at the attorney, and said to him in a flat, even voice signifying total submission to the concept laid before him: "I understand."

Still in deep contemplation, the young man said, "So when I tried out for high school basketball, I wanted to become the best freeshot thrower we had. The problem was that I was really, really bad at throwing free shots! So I set a goal, at least I think I set a goal, that I would practice free throws every day after school for an hour. And, well, I got awards for my free shot capabilities. What you are saying is that the awards did not signify success, at least the real success. If I understand you sir, er, I mean Marv, I became successful when I said that I would not hang out with my friends for an hour; I would, instead, practice my free throws. Success occurred when I made that decision and I followed through with my actions! Yes, I see. Success is progressive, it happens at the beginning of the goal-setting process, not at the end. I remember receiving my first award for free throws. Actually, getting the award was . . . Well, it was kind of no big deal. I guess because after every free throw shot I practiced, I thought about getting the award. It was almost like déjà vu. I thought of it so much, I guess I lived it!"

It was now Huffburg's turn. It was he who was in wide-eyed amazement. Never in the years that he has been coaching young men and woman in the subtle art of goal-setting that a person had absorbed the material so quick.

"Yes, and think about what that change in behavior, that was spawned by your decision to set a goal to practice an hour a day, has done for you over time? It had wide reaching effects in ALL other areas of your life, not just basketball!"

He told the young man, "I believe you have gotten from me exactly what you are supposed to have gotten from me."

Since they were only twenty-five minutes into their discussion, the attorney knew that the young man would have a great deal of time to meet another person who would help him along the path to understanding success. Huffman reached into the pocket of his jeans and pulled out a business card that was folded and creased by the bends in his pants. He said, "Here, it's kind of wrinkled. How the hell would you be if you were in my pocket for an hour?" (Booming laughter.) He began to iron the card between the first and second finger of his right hand and succeeded in causing the card to wrap around on itself so that it became a small funnel. "Oh, hell, just take the damn thing; it's the information on the card that really counts!"

As he handed the young man the card, Huffburg said, "Call this man from your car. He is expecting your call and he may be able to see you today. He will have to give you directions to his house because the card only has his office address on it. I know he's home because it's Saturday and he is a big family man, but he spends a few hours in the morning sewing up some loose ends from the prior week. "

"Who am I going to see now?"

"Someone else who is going to help you on the road to understanding success."

The card read: Sam Pith, Sales Associate.

While reading the card, the young man did not notice that Huffburg stood up and was moving toward the door. The young man noticed, stood quickly, and as he moved toward the door, Huffburg opened it and stood with his hand extended. "Nice to meet you," He said to the young man. "Never, ever stop thinking about your future and about what you can contribute to the world. It is an awesome responsibility, but it's a great deal of fun also!"

The young man thanked him.

The young man left Huffburg's office, pressed the button for the elevator, and turned around to say good-bye. However, the attorney was already gone; he was back in his office, working on a file. The young man grinned and marveled at the intensity of this man who had accomplished so much.

As he got on the elevator, he heard, "Hey!" Turning around prior to the elevator door closing, he saw the attorney standing with an unopened coffee. "You forgot your coffee."

"Uh, thank you."

"No problem. Have a great day, keep smiling, and drive safe. That means don't drink your coffee while you're driving—you'll spill it all over yourself, just like I do." Huffburg said with a smile on his face. (Booming laughter.)

The young man smiled back as the elevator door glided closed.

As the young man entered the atrium, he noticed that there was a snack bar open and some benches near it. He sat on one of the benches, opened his My-Tyme, and wrote:

There is no such thing as "all of a sudden."

Success occurs a day and a moment at a time.

Success is progressive.

Progressive means that we become successful at the beginning of a goal—when we set the goal and modify our behavior to accomplish it.

The young man, closed his My-Tyme, rose, went to his car, and prepared to call the name on the business card Huffburg had given him.

Chapter Two

The young man would have loved to have had a convertible this Saturday morning. The delight of the early morning gave way to a glorious late morning with the sun shining and the sky a deep blue. The air was so wonderfully aromatic that the young man was lost in his blissful thoughts and almost missed his turn-off.

He was not overly familiar with this section of the county as it was very rural and seemed to have a dichotomous population. There were many generations of poor people whose houses were ramshackle and whose yards were so filled with old, rusted cars that they looked like a small version of a junkyard. There were also very well-to-do people with big, rambling houses set back on multi-acre properties.

As the young man was soon to discover, one such multi-acre rambling house belonged to Sam Pith. After leaving Huffburg's office, the young man called the number on the card the attorney had given him. After he introduced himself, the man on the other end of the line, Sam, said that he was expecting his call. He told the young man that he had just gotten off the phone with Mr. Huffburg and looked forward to meeting him. He then gave the young man directions to find his house.

The young man was amazed at the abject poverty he saw. He couldn't believe that people could live in such abysmal conditions, especially in America. When the young man made the turn off the highway, he was shocked to see that it was a dirt road. The next turn was a dirt road also, but even more narrow than the preceding one. He thought that Sam must be a struggling salesman, and that he was sent to him to explain that all goals are progressive and that he will become successful not when he achieves the goal, but when he modifies his behavior and begins to make progress toward the goal.

What he saw in front of him caused him to slow his car down and gaze in rapped wonder. After ascending a knoll, he noticed that in front of him was not just a house but a sprawling, California ranch. Since the road leading up to the home was on the home's right, the young man got a great look at the entire back and side of the home, before the road took him to the front.

He had watched, and was somewhat involved when his mother and father were building their new house some years prior. From that experience he estimated that this home in front of him had to be at least ten thousand square feet—*ten thousand square feet!* And a ranch home at that. The home had a semicircular driveway in light brown cobblestone and the home was finished in light brown brick with a dark brown stone entrance. The roof was dark brown slate, and, by simply counting, he noticed that the home had at least four fireplaces, since there were four chimneys protruding from various sections of the roof.

As the young man pulled around the front door, he noticed a strikingly handsome man with deep, dark golden hair, a cleft chin that jetted out from his smiling mouth showing many, many perfectly white teeth. Had the young man been born several decades prior to his actual birth, he would have guessed this man before him was a lookalike for Kirk Douglas. The man, Sam, was in his mid forties but had a fabulous build. He was standing at his front door with a loose-fitting pair of jeans and a form-fitting golf shirt in one of the brightest pinks the young man had ever seen.

The young man thought, with a smile on his face, "Wow, by the color of that shirt, this guy must have tons of self-confidence."

Sam was washing two of his cars. One that he found out later was a Bentley and the other the young man knew immediately as a Porsche. The young man parked his car and got out, My-Tyme in hand, while Sam, toting a huge grin and displaying dazzling white teeth, extended his hand and met the young man in front of the Camaro.

"Greetings!" said Sam, while briskly shaking the young man's hand, "Have a hard time finding me?"

The young man grinned, thought that this was by far the firmest handshake he'd ever had, and said rather sheepishly, "Yeah, kind of!" While driving through the country, the young man lost his bearings several times and needed to call Sam. Sam skillfully guided him through the arcane back roads with all of their strange twists and jagged turns. At one point the young man felt so utterly lost that he had no idea as to which way to head. He called Sam again and to his dismay found that he had no signal on his cell phone.

Finally, though, with proper instruction, some carful guidance, and enough intelligent initiative, the young man was pulling up to Sam's grand home with some impressive automobiles in front of it, while shaking hands with movie star potential.

"Well, you made it," Sam said as he patted the young man on the shoulder. When the young man had closed his car door behind him, Sam gently guided him toward the front door of his home and asked the young man if he would like something cold to drink.

Even though it was late morning, the sun had already burned away the last vestiges of the morning mist. It was going to be a hot day and sunny as well. Actually, it was already a hot day. The young man was feeling the perspiration form on parts of his body and thought that a large, cold drink right now would do just fine.

As Sam escorted the young man through the front door, he was visually stunned by one of the most attractive women he had ever seen. Sam's wife, named after her great aunt, was saddled with a centuries-old Irish name—Mildred—although everyone close to her called her Millie. Millie was in a strikingly white tennis outfit consisting of a short, but conservative skirt and sleeveless blouse, revealing biceps that have obviously seen the inside of a gym for some years. Her sneakers (tennis shoes) were as white as her outfit and she was completely devoid of jewelry except for her wedding band.

"Mill, honey, this is the young man I have told you so much about. This is my wife, Millie." With outstretched hand, Millie approached the young man with a smile as big and as white as her husband's while saying, "I am so very pleased to meet you!"

I made you some drinks and some light snacks out back. I hope you don't mind, honey," she said looking at Sam. "I set up a little something near the pool. The kids won't be around for an hour or so. If you would like, I can move it all to the den or the library or maybe the studio downstairs?"

Smiling with obvious love on his face, Sam said, "It's fine, baby, the pool is just fine."

"Well, okay then. I am going to kick Mary's ass off in tennis!" Immediately Millie put her hands to her mouth, turned red, and apologized profusely for her slight outburst. She said with a smile on her face that she was very excited about this match and it was truly all in fun. As the redness in her face dissipated, she walked over to the young man, shook his hand again, telling him how much she enjoyed meeting him, then, going over to Sam, she kissed him lightly on the lips, and said that she would see him later.

Sam told her to break a leg and kissed her back. The young man saw that these two people were truly and genuinely in love. He wondered if the complexities of wealth strained that relationship and hoped that he could ask that question later. He knew that his parents were in love, but they were firmly secured in middle-classdom.

He also knew that money had a great deal to do with marital problems. One executive at the corporation, who was doing very well for himself financially, ended up divorcing his high school sweetheart who was a very good businesswoman and owned her own design firm. As their two incomes rose, the problems in their marriage increased in direct proportion. The executive, who had to work with the young man on a special project he was overseeing, had a conversation with him one evening. After a hard day of moving the special project forward, the executive asked the young man, who was the only employee who had "stuck it out" for the entire day, to dinner where he told him about his martial issues. (The executive started with a few scotches and went to wine with dinner.) The result was that both the executive and his wife, having more money than they knew what to do with, had lost sight of the goal—happiness. Instead, they had tried to buy happiness independent of each other.

Both of them had many extramarital affairs, took vacations separately, and lived parallel lives under the same roof. Their constant fighting wore heavily on their three children. Finally, for the mental health of their kids, they decided to split and have joint custody. Both of them, now in stable, loving relationships, were happy that their two oldest children are coming around to the idea that their mom and dad have different spouses. Unfortunately, their youngest child, due mostly to the emotional fallout, became heavily involved in drugs, did jail time, and is now in a halfway house in a different state.

In tears, the executive told the young man that his youngest son had tested out at 152 IQ. He had been active in sports, the Boy Scouts, and was an altar boy. Now, he is hoping to get some training to become a diesel mechanic by changing the oil in large trucks.

"He is changing oil for a living," the executive said. "I understand that his boss is a miserable, stupid, and mean man. My boy has to put up with insults, made to feel stupid, and lazy at the hands of this moron! All because his mom and I made too much money for our own good! Money," the weeping executive told the young man, "take it—take it all, it is definitely overrated!"

The executive stood up, told the young man to pay the check and expense it, and then staggered out of the restaurant, presumably to go home to his loving, stable relationship.

"Hey," said Sam, snapping the young man out of his contemplative trance. "Oh, sorry, I was admiring your home." Although this was a bit of a white lie (the young man had been wool-gathering about the executive from the corporation), he didn't really feel the need to share that thought.

The young man thought, however, that the home was spectacular! Entering the foyer, one was immediately taken by the depth of the house. To his left was a large library with shelves from floor to ceiling. The room also included a rolling ladder, the kind of which is seen in bookstores and libraries. To his right was an even larger formal living room done in black and white—black rug and curtains with white furniture. Modern paintings hung from each wall, all in black and white. Behind him was a great room and two hallways flanked that room, which lead back further.

Sam said, "Well, the love of my life has set up some drinks and a little bite to eat at poolside. Would you like go there now, or would you like the dime tour?"

"Well, I'd love to see your house, if you don't mind. It is really very beautiful!"

"Why would I mind? I *asked* you if you wanted to see it; do you think I would have asked that question if I didn't want you to see my home?"

"Well, I g-g-guess n-n-ot . . ."

"Marv said you were rather obstinate, wanting to call him 'sir' instead of what he wanted to be called."

"Oh. Well, I-I-I—"

Smiling, Sam said, "I am only joking with you! Don't take life so seriously; at least don't take Marv and me so seriously. Take your CEO seriously—he's paying you!"

"Oh, okay. Then, let me rephrase my answer. Yes, I would love to see your home!"

"Better, much better."

As the tour began, he wondered how long it had taken Huffburg to call Sam and if the CEO was at all involved in this conversation. The young man was beginning to feel that this entire day and all eventual meetings were, somehow, pre-orchestrated. He was feeling both excited and apprehensive simultaneously. Excited because of what he was learning (he had learned more from Attorney Huffburg than from most of his colleges professors) and apprehensive because of his fear of making a mistake. He had hoped that he would have the opportunity to speak with the CEO later about these meetings; he would bring it up.

The "dime tour," as Sam called it, lasted well over an hour. The grounds were just as impressive as the house and Sam took visible pride in showing the young man around. Ending in the breakfast nook, which housed the French doors leading out to the veranda and then the pool, the young man looked at Sam and said, "Your house is beautiful, you must be very proud."

Since knowing Sam, which had only been about ninety minutes, the young man noticed a sizable frown on Sam's face. "Proud?" asked Sam, "Nah, not proud, I did it for them." Pointing at a shelf in the breakfast nook, the young man noticed a picture frame that was home to a stunning black and white portrait of Sam, Millie, and their four children. "That's why I did everything!" The young man noticed that the frown had changed to a smile and he thought with amusement, that now, Sam is proud, not about his house, but about what he has created—his family!

As they sat by the pool, the young man was introduced to three of Sam's four children, the other—the oldest—was away at college. When all had settled, Sam uncovered several serving dishes that held some delightful sandwiches, pasta salad, and some iced fruit cup. A pitcher of lemonade and unsweetened iced tea sat next to a serving tray of glasses and a plate of sliced lemons and limes.

They actually spent the next several minutes fixing their plates and glasses. Both men ate with gusto, and only after each of them had consumed half of their sandwiches and a huge helping of each of the salads, did Sam finally begin to speak.

"So, tell me what you have learned so far, aside from the fact that Marv Huffburg is rude, arrogant, and borders on obnoxious."

The young man looked at Sam with a frozen look of wonderment. Sam returned the stare with a solid, impassive face. Then, not being able to subdue his humor anymore, began to laugh. The young man followed suit.

"Well, one of the things I learned was that question-asking may not be as bad as I had thought it was. But, I do need to develop some tact—somewhat in the way Marv has developed it!"

The young man gazed stolidly at Sam whose look showed that he was trying to process that information. Then it was the young man's turn to laugh. Then Sam got the joke, and told the young man, "You got me!"

"I also learned that you don't become successful when you achieve a goal, you become successful at the beginning of the process—when you set the goal and modify your behavior to achieve it."

"Bravo! Bravo!" Sam exclaimed as he clapped his hands in applause.

"Thank you. I guess I also learned that there is no such thing as all of a sudden. I think the corollary is that I need to develop patience."

"Hum," said Sam, "sounds to me as though you have a goal to set!"

"Yes, I guess I do!"

"So, let's say that you set a goal. Let's say that you set many goals. What do we do now? You see, setting goals is easy, for example—" Sam put his hands up, parallel to his body, in mime fashion, "Listen!" At which point Sam stopped talking. As the silence from the country surroundings invaded the area where only seconds ago there was talking and laughter, the young man heard tree leaves fluttering the wind, the sound of the pool pump, several birds, and that was all. These were sounds he would have expected to hear without conversation. "I don't hear very much except for the surroundings."

"Exactly," said Sam. "Exactly. You see, if we talked for an hour or so in this quiet serene environment, and I asked you to start listing your goals, you could do it very easily, couldn't you?"

"I guess so."

"Sure you could. There are no phones ringing or e-mail alerts bonging or cell phones playing their ringtones or anyone in your face at all! I'll bet you could sit here all day and bang out goals that you would love to attain. Then, you go out into the 'real world' again and there are phones ringing and e-mail alerts bonging and cell phones playing and people in your face looking for reports, data, information, lunch, dinner, your time. Whew! I'm getting tired just talking about it."

"You're right."

"And that 'real world' is where you need to start making your goals come true. They have to start happening in that real world where you have a billion other commitments and promises and uses of your time. How do you do it? How do you accomplish what is really important to you when everyone else wants you to help them achieve what is important to them?"

"I don't know!" the young man said with a high level of frustration. "What do I do? What does anyone do?"

"Good question, said Sam, "Do you know what you do? Exactly what Nike tells you to do: JUST DO IT!"

"I'm not sure that I understand."

"Look, goal-setting, goal-setting, goal-setting. That is all we ever talk about to become successful. But, success does not revolve around goal-setting, it revolves around goal-doing! Do you understand me? Goal-doing! Goals have to be realized. That realization is the difference between goal-setting being an academic process and it being a key to unlocking all of the frustrations and inconsistencies in your life. Got it? *Just do it!*"

"I think I understand."

"As long as you only 'think' you understand, let me be clear. You can set all of the goals you would like, but if you don't start to *do* them, well then, it was just a cool exercise! After you set your goals, then you need to act—behave in such a way as to materialize your goals.

"I learned of the GOYA theory years ago. Have you ever heard of GOYA?

"Ah, no."

"It stands for Get Off Your . . . Backside!" Sam said laughing. "Potential without performance is meaningless! All of the muscle in the world means nothing unless you flex it. All the intelligence in the world is unless you use it. Nothing can be substituted for focused action toward the achievement of your goals. Action is liberating; it's cleansing. It is action that cures fear.

"Let me explain: When I was a young salesperson, about your age, just learning the ropes, I knew that I had to cold-call. Normally, if I made about a hundred phone calls, I got about ten live people to speak to. Of those ten live people, I would set up three appointments that would translate into one sale of about $3,000. Do you understand my numbers?"

The young man nodded.

Sam continued, "One day, I spent the entire morning, at least four hours, without setting up one appointment. I was very disappointed, so I made calls during lunch and the rest of the afternoon until six that evening. Not one appointment!"

"Did you talk to anyone, or were you just getting voice mail?"

"Good question. However, it doesn't matter. My psyche was scared and how it happened didn't matter. It's like, well, if I get run over by a compact car or an SUV, I am still run over." Sam laughed at his wit. "Nine hours of calls, more than one hundred and fifty times I dialed that darn phone and nothing. I was crushed. I was thinking that maybe I wasn't cut out to be a salesperson. 'Maybe,' I thought, 'I shouldn't even be in business.' I was down, depressed, feeling sorry for myself. I went home that night feeling very, very low."

"What happened?"

"Well, Millie kicked my ass! She listened to me with sympathy. She nodded when she should have. I thought that she was buying into my misery. When I was finished with my outpouring of self-pity, she looked at me and said, 'Listen, remember GOYA? Well, why don't you follow your own advice? We have two babies in that other room, and another one on the way. I gave up everything for you. You know why? Not because you're handsome. Not because you're smart. But because you're strong. I feel safe around you. I feel safe bringing children—your children—into this world because I know you will protect them and take care of them. But, now, you're acting weak. You're having a bad day and you come home and it's 'boo-hoo me' and 'I'm so sad.' Get your head out of your butt. Get into the office tomorrow and start making calls! That is the only thing that you *can* do. Come on Sam, you know as well as I do—get your attitude right, and the correct actions will follow, and those correct actions will bring about proper results! Positive attitude – correct behavior – excellent results! Sam, you know the script: thoughts – actions – results!'

"'You're right, honey. Thank you for the pep talk. It'll all be better tomorrow.

"'I am glad you think so. Now get ready for bed and let's make some great love. I can feel your third child moving in me, and I want you to feel her, too.'"

"Wow," said the young man, "She is quite a woman."

"You bet. The next day I went into the office. I made a sign for my desk that said:

IT IS ACTION THAT CURES FEAR!

I made thirty-five phone calls that morning, and set up ten appointments! It just so happened that every call I made, I spoke to

24

someone and he or she wanted to see me. Why did that happen? You know what? Who cares why, it just did!

"Look, there are three time frames: past, present and future. We need to use the past as a model for current behavior and we need to plan for the future, but we need to live today, in the present! Too many people live in the past—they look at the present, are not happy with what they see, and they blame events that have already occurred for the present condition. They name it, and then they blame it! Blame is a behavior that focuses on the past!

"Others are afraid of what tomorrow will bring. They assume that the best way not to fail in the future is to do nothing now! Fear is a behavior that focuses on the future. Both blame and fear are limiting thoughts that will negatively alter your attitude and, thus, change your behavior for the worse.

"But, when you use the past as a tool, and history as a model to guide your current behavior, then you are on the way to realizing your goals. When you plan for the future with solid, positive, written goals and work today to realize that future you dreamed of, then you have the proper attitude to make all of your goals a reality. Do you know the best way to not blame the past or fear the future?"

"Well," said the young man, "I guess it means to work now, today—just do what you need to do on a daily basis. When you are busy working on your goals, you don't have time to think about blaming someone from the past for the problems you have today, and you don't have time to fear what may or may not happen in the future. You're doing what you need to be doing today! You use the past to learn from and the future to plan for, but you are realizing your goals today by doing what is necessary on a daily basis!"

Smiling, Sam stood up, grabbed the young man by the shoulder, and said to him, "Get outta here! If you learn any more from me, I'm going to have to invoice you."

The young man laughed, stood up, and followed Sam through the labyrinth that was Sam's house.

As they stood in the foyer, the young man turned around and faced Sam. With raised eyebrows and a curious look, the young man asked Sam, "By the way, I know you are a salesman, but what exactly is it that you sell?"

Sam looked back at the young man appraisingly. "I was wondering if you were going to ask me anything about what I do. I sell consulting services to businesses—processes that help companies and its people get, well, unstuck. I sold a ton of services to your CEO and quite a bit to Marv's law firm also. Frankly, I do very well for myself, as you can see, but remember, it's not about the money! It never was. Every day I wake up and do what I need to do to make the things in my life that I think are important come true. That is my goal! And I will tell you something else, it works! And, it is still working!

"Mark well what we spoke about today! Realizing your goals is freedom. It is the way your life will unfold before you exactly as you wish it to. Don't ever stop believing that the best way to predict your future is to create it, to realize it, exactly the way you want it to look!"

Sam patted the young man on the shoulder and thanked him for traveling so far out of his way to speak to him. He handed the young man a piece of paper with some information on it. The young man read:

Father Joseph, S.J.

Our Lady of Christian Charities Missions and Kitchens

"Father Jo, doesn't have business cards, he doesn't want to spend the money on them. His place is a block away from the corporation's headquarters where you work."

"Ah, yeah, I know the place." The young man said somewhat puzzled. The place Sam spoke of was a broken down building that smelled of old booze and urine. Most of the people who hung around there all day were unshaven, smelly, unemployed alcoholics and drug addicts.

Sam saw the look on the young man's face and knew what he was thinking. "Hey, did you learn something this morning from me?

"Sure I did."

"Good! Do you trust what I said?"

"Absolutely!"

"Good, then trust me on this. Go see Father Jo. You will be there well before one. That is when lunch is served."

The young man looked at Sam with a curious gaze, "To be honest with you, I'm not really hungry. Your wife, Millie, made some great sandwiches and salad, and I'm full."

Sam laughed and said, "Son, you are not going to see Father Jo to eat lunch, you are going there to *serve* lunch! I look forward to our next meeting."

Sam opened the door and walked the young man in silence to his car. The young man opened the door, got in, rolled down the window, and thanked Sam for his time.

Sam smiled, patted the young man on the shoulder once again, turned around, and walked into his house.

The young man left the driveway and realized that he needed a drink; his throat was very dry. Prior to reaching the city limits, the young man noticed a convenient mart with some tables outside. He grabbed his My-Tyme and bought a soft drink, sat down, and wrote under the info from Marv:

Goals must be realized.

Potential without performance is meaningless!

It is action that is the cure for fear.

Just do it!

Learn from the past, plan for the future, but live for today.

Chapter Three

The young man knew exactly where Father Jo's mission was located. He hated walking down that street. Disgusting looking and foul-smelling people would come up to him and ask for a buck so they could eat. A few of the young man's colleagues who worked at the corporation with him told the young man to never give these people money. If he did, they would just spend it on drugs or booze. One of his colleagues went so far as to say that giving them money was like feeding a stray animal—they would never leave you alone after that! While the young man did not like the simile between a stray animal and a human being, his level of detachment to their lifestyle gave him a logical understanding of the comment.

Most of the time, the young man would simply walk away when approached. While he felt sorry for these people, he really couldn't relate to them. They had nothing in common. One time, when he was a relatively new employee with the corporation, having worked there only about a month, he forgot about avoiding "the mission street," as many of the corporation people called it. There was a man—a dirty, unkempt man—sitting on the sidewalk with his back to a rickety wooden fence and a set of steel crutches with arm guides, skewed haphazardly to one side. The man affixed a focused gaze on the young man as he approached, while the young man looked down at the sidewalk in front of him. When the young man was within hearing distance, the sitting man said, "Hey, can you spare a buck for a Vietnam vet?" The young man did not answer. "Hey, can you spare a buck for a Vietnam vet?" When the young man passed the sitting man without answering him, he heard again, "Hey, who the hell do

29

you think you are? I deserve at least a no! I'm the reason you are free and able to go to college. I'm the reason you have money in your pocket so you can take your girlfriend out on the weekend. And I paid the price. Look at my legs—landmines, Cambodia. Nothing left of 'em. Can't walk. And I did it for you and your family. And you walk by me and think I'm dirt! If I could stand up, I'd be right in your face! I deserve better from you, and from America!"

The young man made it back to his cubicle but was visibly shaken for the remainder of the afternoon. Even that evening, his fiancée noticed that he was not his usual self. When she asked him about it, he related the story to her. She listened to him, but at the end asked him what he wanted from her, to listen, or to give her opinion. He said that her opinion would be okay. She said that Jesus said there would always be poor people and that the "haves" have a responsibility to assist the "have-nots." Even though the sitting man may have used that money for drugs or booze, our job is to not judge. Besides, what if he did use that money for food?

While he took all this in, and agreed for the most part with his fiancée, he made it a point to avoid the mission street from that day on. Nevertheless, he never forgot the scene and wondered how America could have let one of its sons fall through the social safety net that we are so proud of.

He thought about this as he pulled up to the front of the mission. He was lucky enough to find a parking space on the street. Then, after some consideration, he pulled his new car around the corner and paid to have it parked in a garage.

As he got out of his car and walked toward the mission, he felt distinctly overdressed. The smell of urine and vomit and alcohol was mixed with the smell of body odor and cooking food. As he walked toward the front doors where people were gathered, waiting for the mission to open its doors, he noticed for the first time that it was not just individuals in line, but families—mothers and fathers with children, some teenagers—were all in line and waiting for lunch. The young man noticed that it was 12:50 and wanted to meet Father Jo before the lunch line started.

As the young man walked to the front doors, he saw that there was a line on both the right and the left, each line slanting away from the double wooden doors, and propped against the building. He walked to the set of front doors and turned the doorknob in the right door, only to find it locked. He tried the left doorknob with the same result.

As he backed up and turned, he noticed the gazes of those waiting in line. He felt immediately uncomfortable, out of place. In a different situation, with "more normal" people, he would have asked if there was an alternative entrance. Instead, he just looked to the right side of the building. Not finding any, he looked to the left and found a side door toward the rear of the building, which was unlocked. Later, the young man realized that he might have made an unconscious association between being poor and being dumb. Just because these people were in need of assistance didn't mean they couldn't think. He felt ashamed.

Walking into the kitchen, the young man noticed a bevy of people working furiously, stirring pots, taking items out of, or putting items into several ovens, preparing salads, and filling pitchers with iced tea mix. Looking and feeling out of place, the young man shambled toward the kitchen hoping that Father Jo would approach him.

He didn't need to wait long. A dark man with curly, jet black hair, obviously of Italian decent but with a set of strikingly blue eyes, dressed in a black suit with a white clerical collar, approached the young man. Without the smile of the attorney or the salesman, this man approached with a firm gaze of intensity—a gaze so focused that the young man wondered if he was going to stop and greet him or just blow right past him as if he were looking for something and the young man was simply in his way.

Stopping abruptly in front of the young man, the priest extended his hand and said, "Hi, you must be the young man Sam told me was on the way over. I'm Father Jo. We have ten minutes before the doors open. In the back near the coolers are some number ten cans of butterscotch pudding. Open them, grab some of the small serving cups, put two tablespoons of pudding into each dish, and place them near that large white sheet cake over in the corner." Father Jo pointed to the rear, right of the building near the end of the food line. He noticed a large coffee urn and saw that it was, if this was a buffet, the desert station.

By the time the young man's sight returned to the priest, Father Jo was gone! He was giving instructions to someone else, an elderly man, in a gold golf shirt, tan poplin slacks, and brown boat shoes. This man, obviously a well-to-do gentleman, listened and nodded, showing Father Jo that he understood the instructions. Within seconds Father Jo swept past the young man again, saying as he fled by, "Chop, chop, dude, the throngs are waiting on us. Scoop the pudding or tell me 'no' and I'll find someone who will!"

The young man snapped to attention and, moving in unison with the priest's steps, he went to the back and found the pudding cans, then did what he was asked. By the time he was finished, the doors opened and a flood of people entered the building, all very orderly and calm. The young man poured a cup of coffee from what appeared to be the largest and oldest coffee urn he had ever seen.

Believing that he had discharged his duties, he sat down to enjoy his coffee. Just then, Father Jo came up behind him and yelled out, "What the hell are you doing? That cake has to be cut, the pudding has to be handed out, one to a person, and I mean one to a person, and, you need to give everyone one Styrofoam cup for coffee. Don't be afraid to tell them to take it easy on the sugar, too. Drug addicts develop a penchant for it! Got it?"

"Ah, yes sir, er, Father, er . . . what should I call you?"

"Father! Now get to work, we have mouths to feed!"

After an hour of nonstop cake-cutting and dispensing pudding and coffee cups, the crowd seemed to thin, but just a bit. After another half an hour, it was apparent that most were fed and all were content. During the lunch, Father Jo, with the aid of a megaphone invited all, passionately, yet with some force, to attend tonight's services after which dinner would be served, assuming they got a food shipment in from a company with an overstock of frozen turkeys. He suggested that all pray for that.

Every few minutes he would say grace through the megaphone for individuals who had recently received their tray of food. And, to the young man's surprise, most individuals waited for Father Jo to actually say grace. He noticed, too, the reverence in their prayers, truly grateful for this gift of food. And, once more, Father Jo's determined and soulful amplified voice filled the room: "Father, all powerful and our ever-living God, it is our duty and our pleasure to serve you. Please allow your people to come together, here in prayer to love, laugh, and give back as they can. Bless us all, our families, and our loved ones. Bless our endeavors both successes and failures. And bless and approve this food, may it nourish us so to build our strength, that we may, once made strong, enter the world again to do your work and be witnesses to your greater glory. As always Father, we ask this through you, Creator of all, your Son, Jesus, who came and taught us how to love and forgive, and the Holy Spirit, whose gifts allow us greater closeness to you, Triune Godhead, for all eternity, Amen."

"Amen. Amen. Amen. Amen. Amen," the crowed murmured back. It was the same grace, said every five minutes for the length of time that the crowd was eating, along with the exhortations about love and not letting problems get you down and admonitions about missing Mass and not praying in the morning or in the evening or making sure that their children are attending CCD (Confraternity of Christian Doctrine class) every Thursday after school.

He didn't sit down or stop talking or stop serving. Actually, the young man noticed that Father Jo, clearly a man in his mid to late fifties, poured every ounce of energy into this lunch and probably did so for every meal that this place served.

Father Jo gave the megaphone to a woman in a nun's habit, not one of the modern outfits where their hair is showing, but one of the old fashioned habits that you see in the movies. It covered her forehead as well as all of her hair. The woman, probably twenty years younger than Father Jo, took the amplifier and Father Jo made his way, with as much energy now as he had displayed prior to lunch, to the young man.

"Grab a bite if you want," he said. "We have to start getting ready for Mass and for dinner, and I don't have a great deal of time. But Sam is on my Board of Directors and a huge contributor to this mission, so I told him I would speak to you today, if you helped serve lunch. You did, and I will now live up to my end of the bargain. Come into my office."

The young man poured himself another cup of coffee since the first one he poured ninety minutes prior was very cold. He followed Father Jo to a battered door that was unlocked.

Father Jo's office, smaller than the area of the CEO's office where he had been yesterday morning, was not only small, but disheveled, hot, and cramped with ancient, battered furniture. The priest went behind his desk and sat in the torn, squeaky chair. Finally, the look of intensity seemed to melt off his face. He seemed relaxed, at ease, content. With lunch behind him, but dinner looming, Father Jo looked at the young man intently. He asked him, "Are you Roman Catholic?"

"Yes."

"Would you like to have your confession heard before we chat?"

"Ah, no sir, I just went a few weeks ago."

"Well, thank God for that. I am sure you committed no sin in the last few weeks. After all, sin is for us mortals who happen to commit them daily. I am sure that a young guy like you with a great job and his whole life in front of him always puts God first and would not think about committing a sin, right?"

The young man bowed his head, understood immediately, and said, "Perhaps a confession would be in order."

"Ah, yes," said Father Jo, "It is so good for the soul. In case you forgot, it starts out, 'Bless me Father, for I have sinned.'"

"Yes, I know. Bless me Father, for I have sinned . . ." The young man, used to a two- to five-minute confession, followed by a Hail Mary and Our Father for penance, was shocked when Father Jo's confession lasted almost half an hour and he doled an entire five decades of the rosary for his penance.

"Well," said Father Jo, "now that we are right with God again, tell me what have you learned from your CEO, the 'Jewish Cowboy,' and Sam?"

"Actually, quite a bit. I think I learned more in the past day than in my last year in college. I learned that success is progressive, it happens one day at a time, and that it has to do with realization, meaning you just have to do it."

"Good, very good. I know you have learned other things, too, and I am sure you wrote them down in that book you carry around with you like a Bible. But you hit the main points. Now let me add a tool to your toolbox of success.

"Let's say that you do change your behavior, and you are making progress toward your goals. Who do you think that success will be worthwhile to?"

"Well, certainly to me! I guess the corpoation, my family, and my fiancée, too."

"Good. Anyone else you can think of that, if you hit your goal, it will be worthwhile to?"

"I don't think so."

"Well, how about me? If you reach your goals and become more successful, would it be worthwhile to me?"

"No, how could it?"

"Wrong answer. And don't answer a question with a question; it's rude!"

"Sorry."

"Look, everything that everyone does affects all of us. By your becoming more successful, it makes me better."

"I don't understand."

"Of course you don't, because you are only thinking about yourself! Reach out with your mind, learn. Did you ever hear of Say's Law?"

The young man, who had minored in Economics did, in fact, remember Say's Law, named after an eighteenth century economist, J. B. Say. It said that supply creates its own demand. "Sure, I know about Say's Law, but what does it have to do with this?"

"Let me explain first in simplistic terms, that of Economics, then, in more complex terms, that of life!"

The young man knew immediately the sarcasm in Father Jo's statement, but decided not to bring it up figuring that the priest had never sat in an Economics or Business course in his life.

 Father Jo continued, "So the university you attended is on the East Coast. Let's say that the university decided to remodel one of its buildings. The contractor they chose bought the new desks and chairs from a local office supply house. The local supply house, which supplies many products from many vendors, called in an order to a Midwest manufacturer of the desks and chairs. The manufacturer bought wood from a West Coast lumber mill. That lumber mill bought wood from a forest harvester in the Pacific Northwest. That harvester sent one of its lumberjacks into the woods to chop down a tree.

"Of course, the lumberjack got paid for his work and while he was depositing his pay from chopping down that tree, he thought about sending his only son to that very university you attended so he could play football, become more successful than his father, and not have to work as hard as he did. You see, by virtue of the university buying furniture, the lumberjack had the ability to send his son to the very university that the order for the desks and chairs came from. That's Say's Law—supply creates its own demand."

The young man, mouth agape, was impressed that a priest, who serves food all day, had the ability to explain Say's Law with such simplistic eloquence.

Father Jo, seeing the young man's look of utter amazement, said to the young man, "PhD, Sacred Theology, University of Rome; PhD, Economics, Fordham University. Magna Cum Laude, both degrees. Impressed?"

"Uh, yes."

"Don't be. It all means nothing if these people go without food!"

"I see," said the young man. "But, tell me, how does Say's Law fit into this notion of 'worthwhile?'"

For the first time the young man saw Father Jo smile. It was a big, delightful smile that made him look years younger. He said, "At last, a good question!" Father Jo winked at the young man, showing that he was teasing.

But, it was the young man's turn to be intense. He didn't smile at the apparent tease, only waited, with rapped attention.

Father Jo cleared his throat and continued, "Think of it this way. You modify your behavior, for the better of course, and begin to achieve new and exciting goals. Now, let's say that I don't know you personally, but I see you around, and I have an opinion about you and how you behave. Then, all of a sudden, I see you change. You are behaving differently. I see you happy, focused, and motivated. I start to see some different results in you because of your changed behavior, and I say, 'Hey, I want some of that. I need to change so I can be more like him, and get more of what he has.'"

The young man nodded his understanding.

Father Jo went on, "Now someone who really doesn't know me except on the surface, similar to the way I knew you, sees me change and he or she changes, and so on and so on. Perhaps you are able to achieve your goal because someone you don't even know, five or ten steps from you, assists you in the attainment of your goals. And it is all because you changed. Your goals are being realized from someone who changed because you changed! Now you see Say's Law in real life!"

The young man grinned in understanding—"The better you become, the better others become and the better you become! Wow!"

"Do you have any questions of me?" Father Jo asked the young man.

The young man thought for a moment then said, "I really don't have a question, but may I tell you a story, and then will you tell me if I understand what you are trying to tell me?"

Father Jo, glanced briefly at his watch, leaned back in his chair, which gave another groaning squeak, placed his feet up on his desk, crossed them, and said to the young man, "Shoot!"

The young man placed his My-Tyme on Father Jo's desk, placed his hand in his lap, and spoke to the priest, "My father told me this years ago, and I think it might fit here. Do you remember a song by Janice Ian that was on the radio years ago titled, *At Seventeen*?"

Father Jo looked at the young man with astonishment, "Sure, I heard that song. I was a teenager when it was out. How do *you* know about it?"

"Well, my father is a great guitar player. He taught my brother and sister and me how to play, and he takes on a few students. He has been in bands since high school and is in a classic rock band now. They play once a week or so for what my dad calls 'bar money.' When this song was popular, my dad was watching a late night show by a guy named, ah, I think it was Casey Kasem. He was some type of big DJ at the time."

"Yes," Father Jo said very matter of fact, "I know the name, and I saw his show many times."

"Well, when my dad was watching this show, I guess Janice Ian's guitarist did a great lead, and the camera did a great job of capturing it. My dad said that he was so enamored with the song, he cried that night. The very next day he went to the local music store to buy his first guitar!"

Father Jo nodded.

The young man continued, "He laughed when he told me that story. He said he didn't know the name of Janice Ian's guitarist, and wouldn't know him if he introduced himself. But, it was that guitarist's skill and practice that inspired my dad to play guitar. That guitarist's movement toward his goal of becoming a great guitarist inspired my dad to develop a goal. He moved forward and he became a good guitarist, and my dad had students who developed goals because of my dad's skills! Can you see the connection? A worthwhile goal once set into motion makes everyone more successful."

Father Jo laughed and said enthusiastically, "Oh yes, I see. And, I am happy to say, that you see, too! I am very, very impressed with you and your ability to grasp these concepts. I need to stay in touch with you."

"Why is that?"

"Because, someday you are going to earn a great deal of money, and I want some of that to feed my congregation!"

Both men laughed.

"One more point," said Father Jo, "just to solidify the point. Do you personally know the pope?"

The young man laughed and said he did not.

Father Jo said that he didn't either. He then asked the young man if he knew *anyone* who knew the pope. Once again the young man answered in the negative.

"Um-hum," Father Jo said. "Here is why modifying your behavior to achieve your goals is so worthwhile: you know me, I know a professor in Rome who was a mentor, and he knows the pope. You are only a few people away from knowing anyone in the world—the world! You'd better set your goals high and behave in such a way as to achieve them, everyone is watching! You owe it to yourself and you owe it to the world. We are all connected and working together for the common good of us all. When you think of goal-setting that way, it's a pretty important process. Don't you think?"

Standing and coming around the desk, Father Jo said, "And now I need to get ready for Mass and dinner." He pulled a card out of his pocket that read:

Senator Phillip O'Brian

Father Jo handed the card to the young man with his left hand, while extending his right hand. The young man took the card, shook the priest's hand, and thanked him. The young man was told that the senator would be at his office until around eight o'clock that evening and the young man should call him and set up a time as soon as he gets back to his car. The young man said that he would do so. Father Jo suggested that he was welcome to come back anytime he wished, or when he felt the need to be of service! The young man said he would. Father Jo placed both his hands on the young man's head and blessed him.

While on his way to where his car was parked, the young man called the number on the card he was given. The senator himself answered, telling the young man he had just gotten off the phone with Father Jo, and that the young man should come by in about an hour. Amazed at how quickly these people seemed to be in touch with each other, he said he would be there. He was further amazed at how late these people seem to work on the weekend. He guessed that success has its price.

The young man figured that the senator's office was only about ten minutes away, which gave him time for a quick meal. As he pulled out of the parking lot, he drove in the direction of the senator's office and stopped at a restaurant he was acquainted with. After he ordered a burger and a small salad, the young man opened his My-Tyme and with pencil to lip, tapping, he wrote:

Success is worthwhile.

As you modify your behavior

and move toward your goals,

it becomes worthwhile to everyone.

Others will modify their behavior

based on perceiving the positive changes

in your behavior.

Chapter Four

Predetermined—
Never Settle When You Can Excel

The senator's office was housed in a modern, clean, yet somewhat modest building with a white brick façade and a royal blue canopy directly in the center. The young man parked directly in front and, as the sun was racing toward the horizon, he opened the glass door and entered the foyer, noting that the senator's office was on the first floor, directly toward the rear center of the entrance.

The young man, with some hesitation, walked through the double doors and entered the senator's foyer. From the open door at the rear of the foyer, where lights flooded out and pooled on the dark blue rug in front of the door, the young man heard a voice telling him to come in. He also heard the spry steps of someone in that office moving toward him with surprising rapidity.

By the time the young man made it to the office door, a man—a rather slim, elderly man—with thinning gray hair brushed back onto his head, and gold-rimmed, oval glasses perched precariously at the end of his nose (a glass-wearer his grandmother would call a "peeper"), smiled a wide smile housing large, shiny, but slightly yellowed teeth. The senator's suit hung on him rather than fitting him. But his overall appearance gave a feeling of wisdom and calmness, as if this was an individual you wanted to be around—someone you wanted to make decisions for you. You felt secure in his presence.

"Ah," said the senator, "I am Senator Phil," as he extended his hand for what would be a warm, firm (political) handshake. "And you must be the young man Father Jo called me about. You made quite an impression on him. That's hard to do!"

"Well, thank you Senator. It is a pleasure to be here."

"I take it you had no trouble finding me?"

"No, not at all, I knew exactly where you were."

"Good. Too bad you couldn't say the same thing about where Sam lives!" The senator laughed while the young man thought about how tight this small network of success-minded individuals were.

Before the young man had a chance to justify his level of astray, the senator said, "Come into my office, let's chat a while. I have dinner and a night on the town planned with my girlfriend, but that isn't until seven o'clock. So, we have about an hour."

The young man looked surprised at the senator's use of the word "girlfriend." Sensing his questioning about how such an "old timer" can have a girlfriend, the senator smiled and said, "My wife—my wife of fifty-five years! I love her so much, I call her my girlfriend. And my girlfriend and I have a date tonight!" The senator smiled. So did the young man. "Now, I am sure you don't want to know anymore about my love life. Tell me, how may I be of service to you on this wonderful summer evening?"

Shifting in his chair, the young man said he wasn't sure, that Father Jo had handed him the senator's business card and said to call him.

While laughing the senator said, "That *is* our Father Jo—a man of few words! Well, how about you tell me, what you have learned so far?"

The young man opened his My-Tyme and said, "Whew, I learned a lot today. I learned that success is progressive, which means that you are successful at the beginning of the goal-setting process, and you change your behavior to accomplish that goal."

"Good, very good. Go on."

I also learned that success has to do with realization—you need to put your plans into action." The senator nodded. "And Father Jo explained to me how success is worthwhile. He meant that as I become more successful, everyone—even people I don't know—benefit from it."

"Ahem. You have been very busy today, my young friend. Let me see if I can add a little bit more tinsel to that tree."

"Okay."

"Did you know that if this great state of ours were a nation, it would be one of the top twenty in the world in terms of output?"

"You mean in terms of GDP?"

"That is exactly what I mean."

"No, I didn't know that. Wow, we live in a big state."

"Well, I don't know about big, but certainly productive."

The young man nodded in agreement and affirmation in the understanding of the subtle distinction.

"Do you have any idea what it takes to steer a state like this?"

"Not really."

"Well, why do you think I am here, in my office on Saturday afternoon? Maybe the Department of Motor Vehicles works Monday through Friday, but I work at least six and sometimes seven days a week! And, I don't know if you noticed, I am not exactly a recent college graduate!"

The young man snickered and said, "Yes, I noticed."

"I will be eighty-five years old this year. I love my job, I work hard, and I am pretty damn good at it. Oh don't get me wrong, the Missus and I get away, and we get away often—a week here and a weekend there. I don't want you to think I am some kind of workaholic who doesn't know how to relax. But, I feel committed to the millions of people who are my constituents. They deserve to know in what direction our state is headed. The way I do that is to know in advance what the direction is. Does that make sense to you?"

The young man thought for a moment about a friend's father, a leader in the young man's boy scout troop. This man, who worked with the young man and his son, was a great man. Other boys in the Boy Scouts always preached that a good scout knows in advance the situation he is headed into. He would always camp or canoe with the boys, but not without checking the weather and knowing where they would stop each night and by what time. He told the boys that the way you have fun in what could be a potentially dangerous situation is to plan it out. Know in advance what you expect, then act accordingly so that those expectations would be met. "Yes, yes, I understand." The young man said. He explained the Boy Scout story to the senator and the senator's nod of approval confirmed to the young man that he was beginning to understand.

The senator continued, "People think that politicians attend fund raisers and kiss babies. The truth is, we want to know what our revenues are going to be a year or two before that money is in our coffers. We want to know what our expenditures are going to be and how that tax money, when applied, will increase the common good of our state. We set up programs and spend your tax dollars well in advance of physically writing the check. Are you understanding me?"

"I, I think so."

"Well, then let me be clear. Success in everything we do is predetermined! Otherwise, you will hit something—anything— and say, 'Yeah, that's good enough! That's where I wanted to be; that's what I wanted to hit!' And that is *bull!* Do you understand now?" The senator was getting loud, but not in anger; the young man saw that it was out of passion.

"I have seen countless people pull an arrow out of their personal quiver, place it in their personal bow, pull the bow back, taut and steady, shoot the arrow, and wherever it hit say, 'Yep, that's the spot I wanted to hit,' and then draw a bull's-eye around that spot. That's just the opposite of what they should do!

"So many people think very hard about their goals, put time into achieving them, but never quite put enough thought into them to see them as they should be once accomplished! What a pity!

"You know, when I was in business and we did strategic planning, we always formed the future right then—in the present—so that the future was planned for. I often wondered why people can't do the same thing personally. It is so simple—know in advance what you want your goal to look like, and then start to apply all of the personal resources you need to accomplish the goal exactly as you want it to look! Your goals need to be predetermined; you need to know in advance what they will look like. How are we doing now?"

The young man smiled and said to the senator, "Got you!"

"Good, good!" The senator said, as he looked at his watch and gave a slight frown. "Uh, oh. I'll have to be leaving you very soon. Can't keep the love of my life waiting too long now, can I?"

"I guess not."

The senator leaned back in his chair, took off his glasses, and positioned them to the right of his forehead. He said to the young man, "Let me ask you this: what is one of the first things you do when you go on vacation?"

"Well, I guess I pack."

"Oh really? And what exactly do you pack?"

"Ah, well, clothes that I am going to wear when I am on my vacation."

"And what *kind* of clothes would they be?"

"Clothes that fit the weather where I am going on vacation."

The senator was silent for a moment, hoping that the young man would figure out this important point.

With a flash of enlightenment, the young man looked at the senator with an understanding gleam in his eye and said, "Of course, I need to determine—*pre*determine—where I am going so I can enjoy myself while I am there!"

"Go on . . ."

"If I am going to the beach, I don't pack sweaters. If I am going skiing, I won't only take tee shirts and shorts. And, the only way I will know what to pack and what to take is if I plan it out in advance! I need to predetermine my vacation."

"Yes, yes, and you need to predetermine your goals for the rest of your life!" The senator said with enthusiastic approval. I do believe you understand. Thinking about your goals and your direction in your life prior to actually applying your resources into the achievement of those goals is one of the most important things you can do in the process of goal-setting!"

The young man agreed and noted that the senator was rising from his chair and the young man followed suit. With agility that belied his age, the senator walked around the desk and extended his hand. After shaking hands, the senator subtly motioned the young man toward the door, saying, "Now, young man, I need to meet my wife for our date. Before you leave though, I would like you to call a certain person. I believe she may be able to put another piece in the puzzle. Her name is Audrey. She is retired. Her husband is dead, but they were both ministers in their hey-day. They were both in the Peace Corps and— Oh, why should I tell you about her, let Audrey tell you herself. Here is her address.

"I am very sorry for the short period of time we had, but one of the most important lessons you can learn in life is not every situation in life will meet your expectations. I hope you got something from our meeting." The senator handed the young man a piece of stationery with the woman's address on it.

The young man noticed, "There is no phone number on it."

"No need. She is expecting you. I hope you're hungry, she is a wonderful cook!" the senator said as he rubbed his stomach and smiled.

The young man knew the street Audrey lived on and knew he would have no trouble finding the house.

"Hurry now. She is expecting you by 7:15," the senator said as he looked at his watch, noting that it was now 6:50. "You can make it with plenty of time to spare; it is only about a ten-minute drive."

The young man thanked the senator as he left the office and entered the foyer of the building. When he got into his car, he opened his My-Tyme and wrote:

Success is predetermined.

You must know what your goals are in advance of applying resources to achieving them.

Thoughtful planning is the key to effortless execution.

Chapter Five

Audrey was a woman, perhaps in her late sixties or early seventies, the young man could not be sure. He surmised that age because of their conversation, but her physical presence contradicted her apparent chronological age.

When the young man arrived at her house, he pulled up directly in front and, toting his My-Tyme, proceeded to ring the doorbell. After several seconds of standing on the meticulously clean front porch and looking out on the meticulously manicured lawn, the front door opened. He was greeted by a slender, well-dressed, red-haired woman in a beautiful, well-fitted poplin dress. Aromas wafting from inside positively assaulted his olfactory senses.

Audrey smiled and the young man took her proffered hand and shook it lightly.

"You must be the young man I have heard so much about recently. Please, come in."

The young man smiled and entered the home, My-Tyme in hand.

He noticed immediately the neatness of the home as well as the modest yet tasteful décor. He also noticed the dining room table set in buffet style and beverages placed on a coffee table near a sitting area consisting of two overstuffed wing-backed chairs.

She motioned the young man to one of the chairs, but his inadvertent glance toward the table, laden with such great-smelling food, made Audrey smile and say, "I guess it has been a while since I have had a hungry man to cook for! Come, join me. Let us eat first, then we can sit and chat for a bit."

The young man, immediately aware of his glance at the table, told Audrey he was sorry, but everything looked and smelled so good, that his stomach had gotten the best of him.

Audrey smiled with reassurance and told the young man that women like to chat and mill around first, with food a distant second, but with men, well, food comes first. "So, let's eat!"

The young man filled his plate with small sandwiches, salads, and homemade desserts. When he was finished, he asked for permission to go back for seconds and was told by his hostess that she would be insulted if he did not. When finished, he leaned back in his chair and said he had never eaten food like that. It was as though it had come from a different world.

Audrey said, "Well, young man, you are not that far off. Some of the recipes came from the South Pacific islands around Fiji. The salads were made from recipes I obtained during my travels in the Dutch West Indies."

"Well, everything was great and I thank you for that wonderful meal!"

Audrey smiled and gave the young man a polite, "You're welcome," leaned back in her chair and said, "So tell me, what have you learned so far today?"

The young man said, "Wow that may take a long time to answer. I have learned so very much from so many different people."

Audrey smiled, but refused to let the question go unanswered. She said, "Why don't you summarize for me?"

"Well, Okay. I learned that success is progressive, which means that you become successful at the beginning of the goal-setting process, when you change your behavior to obtain the goal, not at the end. When you finally achieve the goal, it is as though you have been there already!"

"Go on."

"I learned that success has to do with realization. That means you just have to get things done! Just do it! I learned that success is worthwhile. As you become more successful, it helps the whole world, not just you. I also learned that success is predetermined. That means you must plan your goals out in advance or else any old path will get you to any old result."

The young man smiled, obviously pleased with his ability to summarize the day with such brevity.

Audrey smiled with reassurance and said, "And I guess you are wondering what little tidbit of wisdom I can impress upon you, am I correct?"

"Well, I have learned so much today, I am sure you have some very interesting information for me also."

"Look around you, young man," Audrey said, as she swept her arm in a semicircular motion. "What do you see?"

"Well, I see items from all over the world, I guess."

"Yes, you do! From *all* over the world! And each and every one of these 'items,' as you called them, have special, treasured memories I can sit and ruminate about continually!"

The young man nodded with understanding.

Audrey continued, "Many people who have visited me throughout the years have called my humble abode a museum to my memories.

I smile at that analogy and ask them if they would mind if I changed it just a little bit. I say that instead, it is a monument to my memories! A museum does not conjure the same emotional state as a monument. When I look around, I get excited. When I look around, I get emotional. Ah, when I look around, I know that my life has been successful. The personal effects you see here are truly my personal remembrances of a life well lived and services well rendered!"

The young man's smile faded somewhat and was replaced by a look of bewilderment. He said to Audrey, "I am not quite sure that I understand."

She smiled back and said, "Let me explain. My husband was a Protestant minister who decided during the year we were married that his ministry was to carry him to every far-flung place this world had to offer. He joined the Peace Corps and dragged me along with him! If I am not sounding entirely happy, well, at the time of his decision I was not.

"And, my parents were nearly rabid with rage that this young whippersnapper would have the audacity to take their only daughter and move her away to countries where the only semblance of modern living was an eight-ounce bottle of warm Coca-Cola—once a week! It was bad enough that he was of a different religion, we are Baptists, he was Methodist, but then to take me away to places where I could die—*could die*—from insect bites, bad water, poor hygiene, and debilitated health! Well, my parents, my father especially, would have none of it! He said to me, 'Does this future husband of yours think that he is Jesus himself?'

"But, I loved him! I knew I would follow him wherever he went. Actually, I felt safe with him; I knew he would always protect me. And, you know what he told me many years later? He said he always felt safe with me, too!

"We traveled through all of Africa, many parts of Asia, and even some parts of Europe. Each time we were given a trinket or a token of appreciation, my husband would write about it in a special journal he kept. He called that special journal 'Our Life, as One.' He was always so sweet.

"He explained to me that to be successful, you need to make it personal! You cannot pay to have someone else run the four-minute mile for you. And, as you set personal goals and achieve them, the resulting success is so much sweeter! You see, when you are a young child, your parents set your goals for you—when to get up, when to go to bed, what to eat, what schools to go to, and so on. As you grew older you set your own goals, perhaps what college to attend and where you want to work.

"It is a funny thing about work. Most supervisors set goals for their employees and tell them to hit those goals, just as parents say to young children. The business goals are never personal. If only they treated their employees like adults and helped them make the business goals personal, they would get so much more from their employees in terms of work and in terms of respect."

The young man once again looked confused. He asked Audrey, "How can you make a business goal personal? It's about business; even if you could, would you even want to?"

Audrey looked coolly at the young man and said, "I believe I can answer both parts of that question at the same time."

She continued, "Let's assume you are a manager for a large company and let's say you had nine people working for you. You are handed a big project and your entire department has to work on that project! It may require some additional hours, but since all of your people are salaried, your payroll costs won't increase. Got the picture?"

"Y-yes."

"Okay then. Here is the million-dollar question: is that a business goal or a personal goal?"

Quickly the young man snapped, "Business—obviously it is a business goal!"

Audrey nodded in approval and said, "Young man, you are absolutely correct!"

Then, she fell silent.

Since she was not making any attempt to speak, the young man, beginning to feel uncomfortable with the gaping silence, said, "Umm, I don't quite follow you."

"Nonsense, you answered the question, and I am sure you have some very sound logic to back up your answer."

"Well, then, tell me what does this have to do with success being personal?"

"A good question."

"Thank you."

"Tell me, young man, since this project is going to take a great deal of effort, motivation may begin to wane. How will you begin to create a climate of motivation for your employees?"

"Well," the young man said contemplatively, "I would tell them they are doing a good job and that I appreciate the extra effort."

Audrey smiled broadly and asked, "And tell me, young man, what if they weren't doing a good job? And how many 'Attaboys' do you think you can give before your employees think that you're full of your own 'Attaboys'?" Audrey smiled at her own wit.

"Well, what else can I do? We had this project thrown upon us and we have to get it done. Everyone is just going to have to suck it up so that we can keep our jobs."

"Well, that's motivational, isn't it? Work harder so you can keep your job? Why don't we add: terminations will continue until moral improves?"

Flustered, the young man, with his patience hanging by a string, said, "So, tell me, what would you do?"

"What would I do? I would have anticipated the project a long time ago!"

"I don't understand."

"I would have known my people and known them well! I want to know what makes them tick and what is important to them. I would have taken my assistant manager to the side and say, 'Listen, you know that minivan you are saving up for? We have a big project coming up to work on. Maybe that van may be a bit closer than you think. By the way, how are the kids? First and third grades; am I correct?'

"Now think about that, young man. Look at the difference in our approaches. You said, 'Work harder and you get to keep your job.' I said, 'Work harder and I will assist you in making one of your dreams come true!' Did I take that business goal and make it personal?"

"Yeah, I guess you did, but you are assuming your people will get a bigger raise or something, right?"

"I assume nothing! I *will* fight for my people when I need to budget for next year's salary increases. If my people perform better than average, they should be compensated better than average. I will fight for them in the same way they worked hard for me all year!

And, not only will I fight for them, *they will know* I am fighting for them! So what do you think, young man?"

"Well, I think I just figured out how to make a business goal personal."

Audrey laughed aloud and said, "Let me go a bit further than that: it's *all* personal! Everything we do at work translates into what's in it for me! All motivation is self-motivation, and the best way to get and stay self-motivated is to translate everything you do into a reflection of yourself. If everything you did was that transparent to the world, you would do the best job you could so that the whole world could see how good you are. Guess what? Everything you do *is* that transparent and the whole world can see and you need to always do your best. And, by now you know that always doing your best comes from self-motivation, which is best cultivated by making all goals personal!"

"Wow!"

"And now you can see why my parents were so angry that I married the man I did and left for parts unknown?"

"Ah, no, I am not sure I follow you on that."

"Young man, do you have any idea how hard it was fifty years ago for a woman to get into college, let alone an Ivy League school, let alone have a double major in business and psychology, then go to a second Ivy League school for an MBA? Then, once having finished all of that education, to never really use it in the way it was intended—to make lots of money?"

Laughing the young man said, "I guess not."

"Interesting thing, though—my parents ended up loving my husband, and he loved them."

"How did you ever get that to happen?"

"I told my parents I needed to live my life by my goals, not theirs. That is the way they raised me—to be a free and independent thinker. If I went against my personal feelings, I would be disrespecting them. In other words, I made my goals personal! Ha, I managed my parents in the way they wanted to be managed!"

"And now, young man, if you don't mind, these old bones would like to lie down and get some sleep so that I can do it all over again tomorrow!"

"Do what?" asked the young man as he rose.

"Have another successful day, of course!"

And with a laugh on their lips, they separated.

As the young man sat in his car, My-Tyme opened, he wrote:

Success must be personal.

Always doing your best comes from self-motivation, which is best cultivated by making all goals personal.

All goals, even business goals, can be compressed into personal goals!

The young man, having driven only several minutes after leaving Audrey's house, was surprised when his cell phone rang. He thought it might have been his fiancé asking him how the day went, or maybe even his mother making sure that everything was all right. He was further surprised when he didn't recognize the number on the cell phone screen. He was most surprised when he answered and the fatherly, yet businesslike voice of the CEO said he would like to see him in his office tomorrow morning at nine o'clock sharp. The young man reminded the CEO that tomorrow was Sunday and the CEO, in a flat tone, assured the young man that he was well aware of what day it was.

The young man drove home while wondering what to expect of tomorrow's meeting.

When he got home, he opened his My-Tyme and wrote:

Success is the progressive realization of worthwhile, predetermined, personal . . . what . . . goals?

Chapter Six

The young man arrived at the corporation at 8:15 . By the time he made it to the CEO's suite, it was 8:25 and, not surprised, he found that the CEO's door was open and his lights were on.

In moments, the CEO's doorway was filled with the kindly, yet impassive and intelligent face of the CEO. He smiled and asked the young man to come in.

The young man was not sure how to dress for this meeting and decided that he'd better dress as he did every day for business with a suit and tie. He noticed that the CEO was dressed in poplin slacks and a light green, cotton golf shirt with the name of the country club he belonged to embroidered on the upper left.

"Mary comes in on Sunday morning for a few hours, but she normally doesn't get here until 8:45 or so. When she comes in she will make some coffee. Until then, I can get you a bottle of water, if you promise not to spill it over your crotch or my picture."

The CEO was smiling broadly, but the humor escaped the young man as he said, "No thank you, I am really not that thirsty."

Still smiling, the CEO told the young man to have a seat, which he did—in the exact spot where he was several days prior. The CEO took the same spot where he had been.

"So, tell me, young man, what have you learned during the past twenty-four hours?"

"Wow! I don't know where to begin."

"Normally, you start at the beginning," The CEO laughed, but there was a note of seriousness in his tone.

"Well, I learned that success is progressive—you become successful at the beginning of the goal-setting process. Also, success has to do with realization, meaning that you have to translate your goals into actions and behaviors."

"Excellent, go on . . ."

"Success is worthwhile. That means that if you become more successful by hitting your goals, it helps everyone, not just you. Success is predetermined—you have to plan out your goals in advance and then make progress toward them. And success is personal, which means you have to translate goals—all goals—into something meaningful to you, personally."

"Well," said the CEO, "you have been a busy young man, haven't you?"

"Yes, I have."

"So, is there a common dominator you have learned from each person? In other words, even though each of these very smart and successful people had a different 'take,' if you will, on success. What did each of them have in common?"

"Well, I think each of them spoke of a topic on success through goals and goal-setting."

"Exactly!" The CEO was very pleased and his look of contentment was evident.

"Now that you can see goals and goal-setting are the common denominator to success, let's talk about that elusive subject called goal-setting. Tell me young man, do you think that goal-setting is important?"

"Oh, yes sir!"

"If I lined up one hundred people right across my office floor and asked them if goal-setting was important, how many people would say that it was?"

"Well, I guess the majority—maybe seventy-five or so."

The CEO smiled and said he had done that very exercise with a marketing focus group in the corporation's headquarters to talk about a consumer product they were going to introduce. The CEO told the young man that out of one hundred people who were asked that question, exactly one hundred responded that goal-setting was important.

The CEO then asked them how many had goals and again they all responded yes. At this point, the CEO qualified his question and asked how many of the one hundred had specific, written goals, reviewed them daily, and made constant plans and adjustments for their attainment? The number went from one hundred to two. And, of those two, only one had a goals program to map out his success.

The young man looked vacantly at the CEO and said, "I can't believe that so few people have a real goals program in place."

"Really," said the CEO, licking his lips in anticipation of relishing the look on the young man's face after he asked his next question: "Do you?"

Silence!

Clearing his throat, the young man said, "Well, of course I have goals—I want to get married soon and I want to finish my MBA and I want to move up in the corporation—"

Smiling, the CEO stopped the young man and said, "Stop being so damn defensive. Let me rephrase my question: do you have specific, written goals? Do you work on your goals program daily, and are you tracking the progress you are making in the attainment of your goals?"

Flustered, the young man shook his head and gave the CEO a disparaging "No."

Silence.

The CEO wanted the young man to feel some pain, or at least a level of discomfort. Finally, the CEO said, "Well, young man, get in line. Most people—by my recollection about 97 percent—do not have specific, written goals and are not measuring their progress toward them."

Silence.

The CEO then asked the young man, "Why do you think this is true? So many people find that goal-setting is important, yet so few people set meaningful goals and track their progress toward their attainment."

The young man thought for a moment and said, "Well, I can tell you from my case in particular that I just didn't know how to set goals."

"Good answer, and just so you understand, you still don't know how to set goals! It's not as simple as an afternoon trip to see a few people! But, you are correct in saying that many people simply do not know what to do to set goals. They have never been taught. Our school system teaches math and history and English and science, but nothing about success. Can you think of another reason why people might not set goals?"

"Well, some people may not want to set goals."

"Right again, economic theory tells us about the idle rich—people who are so wealthy that they do not need to work in order to sustain whatever lifestyle they choose. Economic theory also talks about the idle poor—people who are interested in the next recharging of their food stamp card, or their next case of beer, whatever. But these people are simply not interested in setting goals and tracking them."

"Do you think that might be considered laziness?"

"Could be, but I am not a psychologist. Can you think of any other reasons?"

"Well, we said not knowing how to was a reason, and not wanting to was another reason. I can't really think of any other reasons not to set goals."

"How about fear? Maybe some think that if they set a goal and don't succeed that they will be a failure."

"I guess."

"That is called fear of failure, and it is real!" Think about what is one of the surest ways not to fail."

"I guess not to try."

"Yes! And, that is fear of failure. Some people know how to set goals—they want to be more, and do more, and achieve more—but they are too afraid to do so."

"Why do you think that is?"

"Well, I can only guess. I am not a sociologist either. But many people my age had parents and grandparents who grew up during the Great Depression and felt real pain and fear. Many people were afraid of not being able to feed their families! With people your age, many of you may remember the hard times your parents had losing their jobs. Call it downsizing, rightsizing, or reengineering, it's all the same thing—being fired! This memory may cause people to not want to venture too far off the path, and to be happy with what they have.

In other words, they misconstrue that gratitude for their gifts might mean to stop trying for more, as if the universe might think that they were greedy and get mad at them if they continually ask for more. This is truly a shame. These people think that God gave us a governor; but, God put into us a supercharger! We are all designed for more, so much more than what we have done up to now. And, frankly, the universe, or God, thinks that we should always ask for more. The reason is that it has an infinite amount of resources to give to us—they never end. We should always ask for more."

"Wow," said the young man, "I never thought if it that way before."

"Well, I am glad that your eyes are opening up. I heard a very gifted speaker once say that the word fear is actually an acronym that stood for False Evidence Appearing Real. Fear of failure is one big reason my people don't set meaningful goals. And here is another reason: fear of success!"

The young man looked puzzled.

"That's right," the CEO continued, "Some people are afraid to succeed. Their self-image is so low that it simply will not allow them to climb the ladder of success.

"Let me give you an example. A while back, before I was CEO and before I was a VP, I had a very talented employee working for me. This gentleman was a low-ranking employee with no direct reports, but he had the ability to do such great things; I saw it, I felt it! When a new employee started, he would take him or her under his wing and make sure the person understood what needed to be done and how to follow proper procedure. He also explained company policy and did a great overall job; basically, he took a leadership role. And that is exactly what I gave him. I promoted him to supervisor of a section in a department and gave him a corresponding raise to show him I was very serious about his ability."

The young man, fascinated with the tale the CEO was spinning asked, "What happened to him?"

"Well," the CEO stated, "I had more faith in his ability than he did! At least I took it more seriously. You see, all of his former colleagues, the people who now reported to him, started to rib him a little. They started to say things such as, 'What are you going to do with all of your extra cash?' Or, 'I guess you can't eat lunch with us anymore, huh?'"

The young man said, "So, even though you saw great potential in him, he was somewhat stuck behind what his friends thought."

"Yes, he was more concerned about the good opinion of others than in his own career or future. After five or six weeks, he came to me and told me that he did not want to be a supervisor anymore—he wanted to go back to his old job."

"What did you do?"

"I let him. But this guy never made it above the rank and file. It's a real pity. He had such huge potential, but, you know something, young man: potential without performance is meaningless! He eventually retired and has a meager pension. But, he traded away greatness because he would not let his self-esteem grow to the level of his ability. A real pity." The CEO lowered his head while slowly shaking it side to side.

"Okay," he then said, "so, we are asking the question why people don't set meaningful goals. And we came to the conclusion that some people don't know how, some don't want to, some are afraid to fail, and some are afraid to succeed. How are we doing so far?"

The young man nodded but asked, "This whole thing of fear of success really has me stumped . . ."

The CEO thought for a moment and said, "Let me explain it in the terms of a speaker I heard years ago. Both fear of success and fear of failure have to do with what you are concentrating on. Are you concentrating on the achievement of the goal, and all the benefits that will accrue from that achievement, or are you concentrating on something else, like the need to succeed or the penalty of failure? What are you concentrating on?"

The young man looked confused.

The CEO continued, "What if I took a ten-dollar bill out of my pocket and put it on the end of a long board, say two hundred feet long, and three feet wide? What if I asked you to walk across the board and if you make it across that three-foot board without falling off, then the ten dollars is yours? Would you do it?"

"Sure."

"Why?"

"Well, it's a relatively easy task. The chance of failure really isn't that great. I could walk across a three-foot board, even if I was drunk. Err, not that I get drunk often!"

The CEO laughed and said, "Go on."

"The reward isn't great, but based upon the risk, it is worth the action."

"Bingo!" said the CEO. All of our actions are based upon proper motivation. Motivation theory tells us that we do things for one of two reasons: to gain a benefit or avoid a loss. We are constantly making risk/reward choices. Now what if I took that same board and put it across two skyscrapers in the city? I still put the ten-dollar bill on one end. Would you walk across it now?"

"Hell no!"

"Why not?"

"The reward just isn't worth it!"

"Okay, fair enough. What if it was one hundred dollars, would you do it then?"

"No way!"

"How about a thousand, ten thousand, a hundred thousand?"

"I don't think I would. It's just too scary."

"But wait a minute, you just did it when the board was on the floor, why are you so afraid now?"

"I guess it's because if I made a mistake when the board was on the floor, you would just laugh, but I if I made that same mistake on top of the sky scrapers, I would die!"

"Tell me, young man, when the board was on the floor what were you concentrating on?"

"Getting across that board and grabbing the ten dollars."

"In other words, it was the goal and the result of that goal, correct?"

"Yes."

"What were you concentrating on when the board was between the skyscrapers?"

"Falling."

"In other words, the pain and the problem associated with failure?"

"Yes, I guess so." The young man shifted uneasily.

"Now, think about that, young man. It is the same board. When on the ground, you looked at the end result, yet taking that board and adding a 'complexity factor'—an eighth of a mile in the air—you began to focus on something else—the pain or consequence of failure—even though on the ground you could run across that board!"

The young man said, "I think I am beginning to understand."

"Here it is in a nutshell: keep your eye on the ball. Never lose sight of your goal. Never let self-doubt, lack of knowledge or understanding, or the good or bad opinion of others keep you from doing whatever it is you need to do make your dreams become a reality!"

"Wow!"

"Which leads me into the really big reason why people don't set meaningful goals: write them down, then track them . . ."

"May I ask what that is?"

"You may, but I am going to ask you a question and see if perhaps we can back into the answer. Tell me, young man, what do you know about elephants?"

With a perplexed look on his face, and wondering what elephants have to do with why people don't set goals, he said, "Well, I guess they're big."

"Very good. What else?

"Ahh, they're gray. There are two kinds I think: Indian and African." Smiling he added, "They have good memories and they are afraid of mice."

"Ha, very good! But did you ever see an elephant at a circus?"

"Sure."

Mary Popped her head in and said, "Good morning." She added that the coffee was on.

"Elephants are strong also, very strong. If you get to the circus early enough, you can see the elephant moving the tent masts."

Not sure where the CEO was going with this information, the young man said, "Yeah, I guess so . . ."

"Next time you are there, watch the way the elephants are tethered—watch the way they are kept when they are resting. They have a rope tied around their back leg, and the rope is tied to a wooden stake tapped into the ground. Basically, you or I could break free from that arrangement. The elephant, much stronger than we are, doesn't. Why do you think that is?"

"I'm, I'm not sure"

"Because he doesn't think he can! You see, when the elephant was a baby the trainer tied a chain around his leg and hammered the chain into the ground with a six-foot steel pole. The baby elephant tugged, and twisted, and did whatever he could to break free, but he couldn't! After a while, the baby elephant gave up. In other words, he stopped trying—he didn't think he could! When the trainer saw that, he knew that all the elephant had to feel was something tied around its leg and it would think that it couldn't get away or break free, so it wouldn't even try! Do you know what that is called, young man?"

The young man thought back to his freshman days at the university and remembered from his Psychology class that the concept was called conditioning. He told the CEO.

"Yes, exactly," said the CEO. "And like it or not, we are all conditioned to run with the rest of the pack and fly with the rest of the flock. We are told to get ahead and to strive, but not by too much! And everyone is guilty of conditioning us, especially when we're at a young age."

The young man took exception to this. He had been raised by loving parents who wanted him to succeed in every way possible, and he told this to the CEO.

The CEO smiled and nodded while telling the young man, "I agree; you have been raised very, very well and I would love to shake your parents' hands, commend them, and tell them that I think they did a fine job. But, I want you to think about limiting beliefs that can lead into goal-diminishing behavior. When you were very young and your parents were talking with each other, or perhaps had other adults around, and you interrupted, were you ever reprimanded?"

Thinking back to those days, the young man did remember his persistence in question-asking and interrupting, and very many times he was told by both his mother and his father that, "Children should be seen and not heard!"

"Yes," said the CEO, "children should be seen and not heard. What does that mean?"

"I guess it means to be quiet."

"Yes, be quiet or more to the point, 'shut up!'"

Laughing, the young man said, "Yeah, it means 'shut up'!"

"Do you think if you were told 'shut up' enough that it may have an effect on your behavior?"

"Sure. It may make someone reserved and not willing to give his or her opinion, maybe even when it was asked for."

"Yes. And think about this: Mommy and Daddy and preacher and teacher wanted us to get home from school without getting kidnapped, so what were we told over and over again?"

Starting to understand, the young man said, "Don't talk to strangers!"

"Ha. Now think about a new employee's first sales job; what are they paid to do?"

"Talk to strangers."

"Yes, and then ask them for money!"

They both laughed.

The CEO continued, "Sometimes our limiting beliefs can result in less than positive goal-directed action. Much of this can come from conditioning."

"Wow, so I guess we all fall short of succeeding, or at least growing to our full potential."

"Well, wait a minute," interrupted the CEO, "there is some good news here. Perhaps stimulus/response may be difficult to change in animals but we are the top of the phylogenetic chain. In other words, we can change; we can turn that conditioning around and get reconditioned toward greater success orientation through goal-setting. That is exactly the process you are going through now! You are learning to 'recondition'—to 'reprogram' for a greater level of success through the power and process of goal-setting! What do you think? Are you excited?"

"Yes, sure, I am. But I am not sure what this process is that I am going through now. Why is this helping to become reconditioned?"

The CEO was becoming more impressed with the depth of insight this young man before him had. He paused, he thought. He wanted to make sure he expressed his notions of conditioning in such a way that the young man did not think it was an attack on his parents.

After a moment longer, the CEO continued, "There are two ways for us to learn. One way is called impact learning and the other way is called spaced repetition. Let me explain both of them to you. As a child, everyone knows that there is something inherently bad on the top of the stove. Children can't see the top of the stove but they have been told that they should never put their hand on top of it. Now, this information will become imbedded into the child's mind, thus affect his or her behavior in one of two ways. With impact learning, children put their hand on top of the stove and remove it very quickly with burned fingers. They cry and Mommy and Daddy put ointment on their little fingers while telling them that they were told not to put their hand on top of the stove. Guess what: the child learned! Or, the child was told over and over again by Mom and Dad, 'don't touch,' 'hot,' 'ouch,' 'boo-boo,' and their children learned by knowing that something bad may happen if they put their hand up there. By being told over and over again—spaced repetition—children learn. Both impact learning and spaced repetition are learning methods. Obviously one takes longer, but it can be much less painful!"

Both of them laughed.

The young man thought back to his elementary school days and how the nuns in his second and third grade class had him write the times tables over and over again. He expressed his insight to the CEO who responded with, "Yes, I had an elementary school teacher who told me that, 'repetition was the mother of learning.'"

The young man nodded understandingly, and the CEO continued, "These people you are in front of and the next groups you will be introduced to are assisting you with the process of spaced repetition. You could learn goal-setting via impact learning by setting up your goals incorrectly and failing miserably or you can go through the process of learning goal-setting via spaced repetition, which may

74

take longer but virtually guarantees understanding and success. So, shall we continue?"

"Oh yes," said the young man, "I am *very* excited!"

Smiling, the CEO handed the young man a business card. The card appeared to be rumpled and dirty. Upon closer inspection, though, the young man noticed that the card was printed in such a way as to make it look rumpled and the big, dirty thumb print was actually printed on the card also. The young man smiled as he read this very unique business card:

Stanley Shumpski

Mechanical Marvel!

All Auto Repairs Done Here

The CEO asked the young man, "Do you know where Stan is located?"

"Ahh, yes I do, actually; I think my father uses him."

"Excellent!" said the CEO. "I think you will enjoy yourself and learn from him."

"I'm just curious," said the young man, "how do you know Stan?"

"He is responsible for handling our truck fleet and our executive auto leases. He does all the repairs and preventive maintenance."

"You're kidding!" The young man said, obviously flummoxed over the little, greasy, dimly lit garage he had visited with his father, while trying to understand how Stan was responsible for more than three hundred vehicles.

"I kid you not. And he handles my personal automobiles as well. Now, you need to be there by ten o'clock and you are running out of time!"

"No problem," said the young man, "I'm on my way! He works on Sunday, too?"

"Yes, he has a high volume business. Everyone I send you to today works on Sunday when necessary. Many of them, as I, do not feel that work is work—it is a highly paid hobby and an enjoyable process. Sunday is a great day to get things caught up and have some quiet time to reflect as long as it doesn't take you away from more important family and religious activities'. Anyway, enjoy your day!"

The young man had about twenty minutes to get to the garage and knew it was only about a ten-minute ride. He decided to stop for a coffee and he spent a few minutes in his car, sipping the fresh, hot liquid while writing in his My-Tyme:

Success is the progressive, realization of worthwhile, predetermined, personal goals.

Potential without performance is meaningless.

We are all conditioned, but we can change that conditioning if we choose to.

Goal-setting is the most powerful force in shaping our destiny and our future.

(I have not been told this but I feel that this has been revealed to me by all of my contacts.)

76

Chapter Seven

It was 9:55 AM, and the young man was in front of Stan's garage. The place was small, dirty, dark, noisy and, for the life of him, the young man had no idea how this guy could handle the entire fleet of the corporation.

While looking around, the young man noticed that a very large gentleman in a greasy shirt, greasy jeans, and a smile on his face was coming toward him. His hand extended, he said, "You must be the young man the CEO called me about."

"Ahh, yes. Hello, Stan, how are you?"

"Fine, fine, I know your father!"

"Yes," said the young man, "I have been here before."

"I know," said Stan, "I was wondering if you remembered."

The young man acknowledged his remembrance and Stan asked him to join him in his office. The young man followed Stan into an area slightly larger than a phone booth, strewn with magazines, used parts, and greasy rags. While he was appraising the office, Stan said, "Have a seat." The young man was very happy that he had a dark suit on.

Stan said, "When I got the call from the CEO yesterday, asking me to meet with you today, I said, 'Sure.' After all, you don't disappoint your biggest customer." Stan laughed and it was a thunderous laugh, reminding the young man of Attorney Huffburg's laugh from a day ago.

The young man smiled also. He still could not help wondering how Stan was able to manage so many vehicles in such a small and unorganized shop. Stan, apparently reading the young man's thoughts, said to him, "Come with me," and stood up. Walking out the door and toward the back of the shop, the young man followed him.

At the back of the shop was a door, Stan entered and the young man followed him into an extremely large, modern, and very clean and brightly lit auto mechanic facility. There were many workers in uniforms working on several of the corporation's delivery vehicles that the young man had recognized. There were several offices along the right side of the building that contained individuals with clean uniforms yet these individuals wore ties. As Stan walked by each of these offices, each of the men within them looked up, smiled and greeted him. Stan returned the greeting.

Stan turned, looked at the young man and said, "This is where I handle the corporation's vehicles and the five other large accounts I have. This facility handles approximately three hundred vehicles per week." Stan's demeanor changed, the young man noticed. He became more focused, more businesslike. The young man noticed a distinct similarity between Stan and the CEO. He thought that even though Stan was still dressed in old greasy clothes, and may not look like a traditional executive, he really is. He emanates that image, not physically, but mentally.

At that moment, a young man approached Stan. He was dressed in a shirt and tie, and a pair of clean slacks, neatly laundered, yet there was no doubt they were designed as part of a uniform that got dirty. He said, "Excuse me, Stan. We have a bit of a scheduling dilemma." Stan interrupted his employee and said, "I know, I got it under control. I was going to tell you not to worry about it; I'm sorry it took me a while to get to you." Stan's employee smiled and said, "No problem, Stan, thank you." Stan smiled back and gave his employee a hardy, "You're welcome."

It was obvious to the young man, after observing Stan in action, that he was a good businessman—a very good businessman.

Stan told the young man to follow him. Both of the men walked to the back of the meticulously maintained garage. Stan opened the door in the back center of the structure, walked down a carpeted hallway, and opened one of two large wooden doors at the end of the hall. Both men entered into what the young man immediately saw was Stan's private office. While the office was not as spacious or as lavishly adorned as the CEO's office, it did project power, success, and hard work, but, in the spirit of blue collar modesty. There was no question in the young man's mind that Stan was a self-made man.

Stan directed the young man to a chair in front of his desk. The young man thought that Stan was going to sit behind the desk. Instead, he positioned himself next to the young man in the twin chair next to where the young man sat.

Both men looked at each other for a moment. Stan smiled and said, "Well, now, I understand that you completed your first leg of the CEO's excursion, how did it go?"

The young man, slapping the palm of his right hand against his forehead said, "Wow!"

Stan smiled and said, "Yeah, I know just what you mean! But you learn, man, do you learn!"

"Yes," the young man said, "It is all about learning—learning about success, goal-setting, personal management—"

"Life," injected Stan, "You are learning about life and how to build a profitable, enjoyable life in the exact terms you are looking for. You are in control, young man. You are the driver of your life. Can you feel it? Do you understand what I am saying to you?"

"Yes, at least I think so."

"Look," said Stan, "there are only two types of people in this world: champions and victims. Champions are people who set their goals, write them down, and make plans—specific plans—to attain them. In other words, champions are the main actors in their own goals program. Victims, on the other hand, are in someone else's goals program. They accept the scraps that the champions drop from the table and say, 'That's good enough for me.' Victims accept handouts, do what others say, and never lift their heads high enough because they are worried about getting shot. But in the process of metabolizing their fear and not lifting their heads, they can't see! They never look up far enough to see! What a travesty, what a waste of God's talent!"

With an amazed look, the young man said, "I guess I never heard it put that way before."

"Well," Stan said, "I am not much at mincing words. Basically, you are either in your own goals program, or you are an actor in someone else's. Which is it for you, young man?"

"I want to be in my own goals program!"

"Good, very good! I know you realize that success is the progressive realization of worthwhile, predetermined, personal goals. That's what you learned yesterday, right?"

"Yes," said the young man.

Stan continued, "Now, let's talk about that last word. Let's talk about goals. There is one way, and only one way, to set goals." Stan grabbed a sheet of paper and in his big, scrawling handwriting wrote this:

SMART(T)

While saying, "Goals need to be smart—SMART! Smart! Now, what is the word SMART?"

"Well, I guess it is an acronym."

"Exactly," said Stan. "Do you have a lot of acronyms at the corporation?"

"Oh yes," said the young man, "more than you could imagine!"

"Yeah, I do here, too. I want to reduce the amount of acronyms in use so much. I started an organization to limit the use of acronyms."

Amazed, the young man said, "really?"

"Yes," said Stan smiling, "it is called the Acronym Suppression Society, or ASS for short!" Stan's laughter was booming! It was obvious he had told this joke a million times and took great pleasure in it. The young man was not sure which he enjoyed more, being baited by Stan and brought into the middle of his little jest, or Stan's obvious sense of being pleased with himself. In either case, the young man knew that he liked Stan. He liked him a lot!

"Anyway," Stan continued, "guess what we are going to go over today?"

"The young man smiled broadly, knowing the answer, "I guess I am here to learn what the 'S' is, right?"

"You go it." Stan said with an equally broad smile on his face. "By the way, do you know what the opposite of a SMART goal is?"

"I don't know. A dumb goal?"

"No," Stan snapped. "The opposite of a SMART goal is no goal! None! Do you understand?"

"Not really," The young man said.

"There is only one type of goal—a SMART goal. If the goal isn't SMART, it is not a goal. Does that make sense now?"

"Yes, but I am not sure what SMART stands for." said the young man.

"Okay, fair enough. Let's begin," Stan said as he crossed his legs and arched his back in the chair. "Let's talk about the 'S'. Listen closely, young man, because I don't like to repeat myself. For goals to work, first and foremost they must be specific. Specific. Get it?"

Before the young man had a chance to answer, Stan continued, "How can you aim at something and hit it if you don't know what it is?"

The young man interrupted Stan saying, "You can't."

"You're right! You can't! Goal-setting is like a rifle shot, not a shotgun shot. As a matter of fact, it is more like a laser beam. Goal-setting must be focused, deliberate, and a matter of the mind. But, goal-setting also needs to be exciting, fun, exhilarating, and motivating. However, setting specific goals is serious business! You need to answer a lot of questions."

"Questions?" said the young man. "Like what?"

Stan leaned back in the chair, his bulk making it creak and moan, and said, "Think first about the *what* question. You need to ask yourself, 'What do I want to accomplish?' Is there a *where* question that needs to be answered? In other words, does the accomplishment of a goal require a specific location? Hey, if your goal is a vacation, you'd better know where before you buy the plane ticket!

"Also, there may be a *who* question that needs answering. Are other people involved? If you set a business-related goal and to accomplish that goal you need information from other managers, you need to identify them. *When* questions are important, too. That involves timeframes, but you will hear more about that later today. Perhaps there are *which* questions. Which resources might be needed to accomplish what you want to accomplishment. And don't forget about the *why* goals. Think about it: why do you want to accomplish the goal? Is it for money, fame, glory, prestige, promotion, and love—whatever? Also, we need to look at the *how* goals. How will you put it all together?"

"Wow," said the young man, "That's pretty deep, but very thorough!" The young man looked at Stan with a level of questioning contemplation and said, "So, people are either champions or victims?"

"Yes."

"Either we are in our own goals program or a tool in someone else's, right?"

"Right."

"So, until I make it to CEO, I am a tool in someone else's goals program, right? I guess all employees are in someone else's goals program. Their bosses and all business owners are in their own goals program, ahh, right?"

"Wrong! No! Absolutely incorrect!"

With a puzzled look, the young man said, "Why? I don't understand."

"You are suggesting that goal-setting is only for the lucky few who open up a business or make it up to the highest levels of the corporate world. Follow me!"

Stan got up, brushed past the young man in a way that beckoned him to follow. Once outside the office and back in the large garage, Stan looked around for a moment, found the person he wanted, and with an, "Ah, there he is," continued to move forward with the young man behind him.

·On a dolly, under one of the corporation's vans were the legs and boots of an individual; the rest of him was hidden by the vehicle. Stan said, "Norm, roll out here for a minute."

Immediately, the legs and boots began to move forward and the rest of a man, older than the young man, but younger than Stan emerged. He stood up, smiled at Stan, and extended his hand toward the young man smiling. "Hi," he said. "My name is Norm."

Stan said to the young man, "Norm here is one of my best mechanics, and a fine employee. Say, Norm, how old are you?"

"I'll be forty-five next month."

 "Tell me about your long-term goals, will you?"

"Well, my wife and I want to retire to Colorado in the next ten years. We love to ski, the kids will be grown and gone, and that is what we want out of life."

"How much do you think you will need to retire?"

"I'd say about two million dollars."

"How are you doing with that amount?

"Well, I have just over a million saved now. My wife is an RN and she works as many shifts as she can. I rework old car parts and sell them on eBay and tend bar one night a week. Our kids are well provided for, but we don't spoil them, neither do we have many luxuries. The end result is that we spend good quality time with our kids, but it doesn't cost a lot. With all the money we make, we save between $1,500 and $2,000 a week. In ten years we should have about $2.8 million with the interest. When we finally do buy that condo in Colorado, I should have enough left to open a small boutique garage catering to expensive autos. With the interest from the remaining money, I should only be working three days a week, the rest of the time should be spent on the slopes."

"Wow," said Stan, as if this was the first time he heard the story, "Sounds like you have your goals pretty well in hand."

"I do."

"So, how do you view our relationship?"

"Well," said Norm, scratching his chin, "I guess I do the best job I can for you. You pay me well and give me as much overtime as I can handle."

"So, is it fair to say that you are using me to achieve your goal?"

"Damn straight!" said Norm. "I want to retire and I am using this job as the means to get there."

Stan patted Norm on the back and said thanks to him, then, asked the young man to join him back in his office.

Once in the "sanctum," Stan asked the young man, "So what have you learned?"

Smiling a deep introspective smile, the young man said, "I guess we are all tools in someone else's goals programs."

Stan said, "Hey, I ain't no tool!" They both laughed. Stan said, "But we are all dependent on each other, now, aren't we?"

"Yeah, I guess so." The young man thought how odd it was to sit in front of this overweight, middle-aged man in greasy pants and shirt, yet hearing him speak like the CEO.

"But," said Stan, "let's get specific. What does Norm want to accomplish?"

"Retirement by age fifty-five."

"Who is in his goal?"

"Well, you are, Stan. And then Norm and his wife. Maybe a realtor in Colorado."

"Good. And, we know the answer to the where question?"

"Colorado."

"And, we know the option to the when question?"

"Ten Years."

"How about the answer to the how question?"

"Well, I guess it revolves around hard work, saving money, and staying focused."

"And what about the answer to the why question?"

"So that he and his wife can follow their passion—skiing—and retire young and comfortably! Hey, how did I do?"

"Great, young man, absolutely off the chart!"

The young man began to think about the notion of specific goals. While lost in his thoughts, Stan said, loud enough to snap the young man out of his contemplations, "Mutual dependence! That's the key to life—and goal-setting. Like it or not, young man, you can't do it all yourself! But that mutual dependence is based upon specific, written goals! Listen closely: Your goals need to be specific! Ask those simple questions and get your goals specific! Got it?"

"Got it!"

"Good. Now get the hell outta here. I got corporation cars to fix, and if I don't, your CEO will have my ass!"

Both men laughed, shook hands, and on the way out, Stan handed the young man a business card with a huge, greasy thumb stain on it. At once the young man remembered Stan's card, and the young man said to Stan, "Oh, thank you, but I have one of your cards."

Stan said, "I know. This isn't my card."

Perplexed, the young man at once thinking that Stan is sending him to see another mechanic, looked at the proffered card and read:

Sidney Solum

Stock Broker

Stan immediately knew the reason behind the young man's confusion and said, "Sid's a great guy. Sorry about that—the thumbprint is mine!"

Laughing, the young man said, "No problem. Is he waiting for me now?"

"Well, you are about twenty minutes from his office, and he is expecting you in about an hour, so you have some time to kill."

"Thanks again."

"My pleasure, young man."

The young man drove to a local donut shop on the way to the downtown district of the city. Although he eschews donuts because he views them as unhealthy, he did enjoy the store's coffee. As he sipped the piping hot liquid, he wrote in his My-Tyme:

Goals need to be specific.

To get your goals specific you need to answer the

What, Who, Where, When,

Which, How, and *Why* questions.

Specific goals are mutually dependent. Everyone needs to work together to help each other with their goals.

Chapter Eight

Measurable—
If You Can't Measure It, You Can't Manage It!

The office of the brokerage house was on the same block as the corporation's headquarters. It occupied the top three floors of one of the most impressive buildings in the city.

The young man entered the top floor from the elevator five minutes prior to his appointment time and was greeted by an extremely thin, gray-haired gentleman with round, wire-rim glasses that lay precariously at the tip of his nose. He wore a pair of light brown poplin pants and an off-white button down shirt, both meticulously pressed. The gentleman was smiling broadly, and before the young man could ask about his next appointment, the elderly gentleman extended his hand and said, "Hello, young man, my name is Sid—Sid Solum. I've been expecting you. Please join me in my office where we may converse for a time."

The young man, noticing how quiet the office was due to it being Sunday, followed Sid to a corner office comprised of two sides of floor-to-ceiling windows, bright off-white walls, carpeting, and some of the most striking modern furniture the young man had ever seen. It took his breath away.

Sid walked over to a low, wrought iron bistro table, flanked with two wrought iron chairs of the same design. Sid, still smiling, asked the young man if this seating was acceptable to him. When the young man answered in the affirmative, Sid asked him, "Would you allow me to serve you a bottle of cold spring water or perhaps a soft drink or maybe a nice fresh cup of coffee?"

"Ahh, well, I guess water is fine."

"Very good." Sid walked behind his desk, opened the bottom of his credenza, which housed a small refrigerator. He removed a bottle of water. He turned toward the young man and asked if he would like a glass and some ice. The young man answered no and Sid brought the vessel over to him and placed it on a small cork coaster that was already on the table. He went back to his desk and took his mug of coffee; walking back to the table, he placed it on another coaster, and lithely sat in the chair near the young man. "What a gloriously day *it* is," he said.

Sid placed the accent on the 'it.' Sensing that it was a question, the young man responded that it was, while Sid looked out the window, smiling, with a look of reposeful contemplation.

"So, tell me," said Sid, "What have you learned so far?"

"Well, I learned so very much; but I guess what it boils down to is I learned a definition of success—goals need to be SMART! Stan told me about the 'S' in smart, and handed me your card."

Still smiling, Sid asked, "And why do you think you're here?"

Now, smiling back, the young man said, "I suppose it is to learn the 'M'!

Laughing a thin, strained-sounding, yet genuine laugh, Sid said, "Yes, today we will be conversing about the 'M'!"

The young man, smiling back asked, "Does the M stand for meaningful, as in meaningful goals?"

Smiling broadly, and looking directly into the young man's eyes, Sid said, "No!"

The silence was somewhat uncomfortable, then Sid continued, "The M stands for measurable. You see, young man, goal-setting is like wealth creation, if you can't measure it, you can't manage it! Think about it, what if I called my accountant and asked him what my net worth was, and he answered, 'not bad, you're doing okay.' What did that tell me?"

"Well, nothing."

"Precisely. Nothing! The answer should be, 'Well Sid, your net worth is $1,350,000; it is up 2 percent since the beginning of the year and 4.5 percent year over year.' Now tell me, young man, is that measurable?"

"Oh yes!"

"Do you think I can use that information to manage my wealth?"

"Sure."

"How about with the first example?"

"Well, no, you didn't get any information."

"Exactly. When the measurement component of goal-setting is missing, you don't have any information so how can you manage the outcome?"

"You can't."

A look of content went across Sid's face as he continued, "You weren't born when this happened, but I can remember the first man landing on the moon. Do you know what I heard about the capsule that took those brave souls to the moon?"

"What?"

"That the capsule was only dead set on the moon heading for its target only 4 percent of the time."

Confused, the young man said, "I don't understand, where was it heading the other 96 percent of the time?"

Raising the volume of his voice slightly, Sid exclaimed, "Jupiter! Maybe Mars or Venus—"

As Sid's voice trailed off, the young man began to understand, "You mean it wasn't on track, don't you?"

"That is exactly what I mean, and if the correct measurements were not taken, and compensatory actions taken based upon those measurements, the astronauts would have missed the moon! Also, they needed to make those compensatory adjustments early. The longer they waited, the more fuel they would use to get back on track. You see, if you can't measure it, you can't manage it!"

"Yes, yes" the young man extorted excitedly, "I see!"

Sid continued, "Some measurements are easy because the goals are easily trackable. For example, let's say you want to go on vacation next year. The trip will cost you two thousand dollars, so you need to save forty dollars per week. The first week, you have forty dollars saved, and you know that you have one thousand, nine hundred and sixty dollars to go. Your goal is trackable, therefore it is manageable. So if one week you miss your forty-dollar payment, you know you need to come up with eighty dollars next week. If you don't do that, well, then your trip might be in jeopardy, requiring you to either change your timeline or abandon the goal completely!"

"Wow," said the young man, "you do come right to the point!"

"I handle several billion dollars for my clients. They expect me to make them money—more money than they can make anywhere else. For as close as I am to my clients, if they can make more money elsewhere, that is where they will go. I need to be direct and plain. My clients are like that. When I make money for my clients, I call and celebrate. I then advise them on how they can take their new wealth and invest it to make even more. When money is lost, I call my clients quickly and let them know in direct terms exactly what happened, why it happened, and what we can do to mitigate the losses to the best of our ability. You see—right to the point. I know the goal, I know how to measure the goal, and I can take action based upon the information I obtain from that measurement."

Sid continued, "But, young man, you need to understand that some goals are very difficult to track. Think about how you measure goals, about increasing level of patience or productivity, controlling your temper or being a better listener."

A look of concern covered the young man's face. He said, "I, uh, was getting really excited about tracking goals, but I never thought about goals you can't track! What do you do?"

Sid said, "There are two goals: tangible and intangible. Tangible goals are very easy to measure, intangible goals are not. However, you can measure intangible goals; it just takes a little creativity. Unfortunately, it is beyond the scope of this meeting to cover that topic. I think you will need to speak to the CEO about that!"

Sid's smile was unwavering as he said, "Don't be discouraged. Don't think about what you don't know; think about what you have learned! And, young man, you have learned a great deal. Are you beginning to understand?"

"I understand how important measurement is to goal-setting."

"Of course you do, my goal was to explain this concept to you as succinctly as possible in twenty minutes. We finished in twelve minutes, so I have eight minutes that I can invest in my business and earn more money, but since I am turning eighty this year, I think I will invest those eight minutes in savoring my cup of coffee.

The young man smiled.

Sid rose and told the young man that they would meet again and very soon.

The young man rose also, shook Sid's thin hand, and thanked him for his time.

Sid was in the process of saying good-by, when he exclaimed to the young man, "Oh my gosh! I almost forgot to tell you what your next stop is! I guess I might be getting old!"

Sid reached into his pocket and took out a rather unique business card. It read:

Sew Right!

Custom Dresses by Michelle

The reason the card was unique was because the letters were embroidered on an off-white piece of linen fabric. The young man took the cloth, and rubbed it between his thumb and first finger. He felt the raised letters of the embroidery and was thinking about the great marketing appeal of this type of business card when the soft, yet persistent and professional voice of Sid broke his concentration.

Sid asked the young man, "Do you know where Shelly's storefront is located?"

The young man frowned because the address did not look familiar to him. "No, I can't say it rings a bell."

Sid laughed and said it was on the first floor of this building. He went on to say that Shelly did not put the building name on the card so that people would have to think hard about her location. Sid said that many people call Shelly for directions and once they find out she is on the first floor of one of the city's landmark locations they ask why she doesn't include that tidbit of useful information on her business card. Her response is that if she did, they would not be talking right now and she would have lost the opportunity to speak to such a nice person in advance.

The young man voiced his question about the validity of that marketing strategy and Sid suggested that he go down the elevator, find her retail store, and ask her. He might be very, very surprised! Sid also suggested that the young man should hurry. She was normally very busy on Sunday with appointments and found that she needed to close between noon and 12:30 so she could grab a bite to eat and think about life for a while. Shelly was waiting for the young man. Sid said that she had lunch for the two of them.

Walking the young man to the elevator, Sid thanked him for his time and attention. The young man said that he should be thanking Sid instead. Sid said that the young man could thank him later because they *will* be meeting again very soon.

On the way down the elevator, the young man, standing and balancing his My-Tyme in his left palm, while writing with his right hand, wrote:

Goals must be measureable.

If you can't measure them,

you can't manage them.

Measurements give information

you can act upon.

Chapter Nine

Attainable—I Do Believe That I Do Believe

The young man found the retail outlet, which was facing the main street. He was surprised that he had never noticed the store before. The windows were done up with mannequins without heads. Most of the bodies were long and slender, and adorned with some very unique colors, styles, and fabrics that combined to make dazzling dresses. The ambiance was traditional summer—vividly colored flowers, green leaves, yellow to emulate sunshine. It made the young man feel happy, optimistic, and want to bring his fiancé to Shelly's to buy a dress. Then he thought about his concern about not placing the building name on her business card. He thought, "How many people would simply walk in and not look in the window?"

It was right around noon when the young man walked into the store when what seemed to be a whirlwind appeared almost out of nowhere. She approached the young man with a rapidity that was somewhat frightening.

Standing in front of the young man was a medium-built woman in her mid-thirties, brown hair, with bangs that came to her eyebrows, sporting rectangular, brown glasses. She wore a baggy sweater and polyester pants, both a muted earth tone, and both with pulls and frays that affirmed either their age or their usage.

Shelly was not simply smiling at the young man, she was beaming! Her smile comprised of strikingly white teeth and lovely, soft lips that stretched taunt across her mouth. Shelly was a charming lady. That charm emanated from her.

After shaking the young man's hand and saying hello, she swept by him, turned the open sign to the side that said "Back at 12:30," and locked the door. Still smiling broadly she said to the young man, "Oh, I love my work, I absolutely love it, but if I don't take thirty minutes to eat lunch and think about life, I will go crazy!" The word "crazy" came out elongated and in falsetto. "Turkey or tuna?"

"Ah, excuse me?"

"I bought two sandwiches. I didn't know your preference since I didn't know you, so I bought a turkey and a tuna sandwich. Both are on whole wheat, both have a big, juicy dill pickle half and both are beyond delicious! I love them both so I don't care which I eat. They come from the Jewish deli next door.

"Now, we don't have a great deal of time. I open back up at 12:30 and I will have several people waiting at the door. We have spent more time talking about sandwiches than we should, given the limited time available to us. So, pick a sandwich, sit down, and eat!"

"Tuna."

"Good, here, eat."

They sat in a very small area in the back of the store separated from the front by a trifold wall of oriental décor.

As Shelly talked through her turkey sandwich, she asked the young man how his time has been going. He told her about the amount of information he had acquired during the last two days but he noticed that he was speaking very rapidly. The young man had absorbed her sense of urgency. He felt her authority. He knew that Shelly may come across as an artist, a seamstress, and a hard worker. She was all three, but she was also a very powerful woman who had the ability to contort another person's will by the sheer force of her personality. Yet she did it in such a disarming, friendly way that people knew they were taking on Shelly's demeanor though they really didn't mind. She was that powerful, yet that nice of a person.

She continued, "So, what shall we talk about today?"

The young man responded, "Well, I guess we are going to be discussing the 'A' today."

Smiling broadly, Shelly said, "Yes, we will be discussing the 'A'. Normally I would ask you a few questions, but we are rushed today, so I'll tell you. The A stands for attainable. Do you have an idea as to why that word is part of goal-setting?"

The young man said, "Attainable? Hum, that means reachable, right?"

"Normally I would agree with you, but in the context of goal-setting, attainable takes on a slightly different meaning. I would say that the synonym for attainable, with regard to goal-setting, is believable. And would you care to venture a guess as to who the goals need to be believable to?"

"Sure. Goals need to be believable to the person setting them."

"That is right on the money. If you don't believe in the goal, or believe that you can reach the goal, there is a very good possibility that you will not hit it. When I was in the corporate world, during the first few years I was out of design school, I would see managers call employees into their office for their yearly review and tell the employees what their new goals were for the coming year. The employees would accept because they didn't think they had a choice to, and then they would leave the boss's office and wonder how the hell they were ever going to hit that goal. The manager felt comfortable because the employee said that all was good. Then, several months into the New Year, when it became apparent and painfully clear that the employee was in no way going to hit the goal, the manager would meet with the *manager's* boss to discuss the future of this employee because he or she obviously could not do the job properly.

"I wonder, young man, I really wonder: how many employees have been fired because their boss has rammed goals down their throat, never allowed them to give an ounce of input into the goal-setting process, or give them an iota of assistance or help in achieving the goal?"

"Yes, I see your point. The employee never thought of this new goal as being believable so the chances of hitting it were slim."

"Exactly. Not only didn't the employees not believe it possible, their boss didn't even give them the respect of asking if the employees thought it was doable. And this doesn't happen just at work, either. How many parents make their kids play baseball when they would rather be reading? Or reading when they want to play their guitar? How many parents set unreasonable goals for their children and, in the process, lose balance? Now, you might be thinking, 'Come on now—all kids need to read and do homework.' No question there, but they also need to play with their friends and walk in the woods and go swimming and sing and dance and be happy! And, to be sure, while all kids should have other activities to keep them occupied, they need to spend some time—actually a lot of time—doing their homework, too. And, did I forget to mention quality time with Mom and Dad?"

"Well," the young man asked questioningly, "what would you suggest bosses and parents do?"

"A very good question. The answer is communication. Is it really that hard for a manager to ask their employee a week prior to the review to come up with some goals for the next year, and the boss would do the same? Then, when the boss and employee meet, they can negotiate the goal. Sure, managers need to have their goals achieved, but, what good would it do if employees simply fail or, worse yet, quit without the goal being hit? The goal would still not be completed, so why not work with the employees? Same with parents and kids. Isn't it better to sit with your child and work out homework time, and Boy Scout time, and football time, and goofing off time?"

"Yes, sure it would."

"With communication comes buy-in, with buy-in, comes believability!"

"I see," said the young man, and he really did see. He understood Shelly very well.

Shelly continued, "Look at this place, would you?"

The young man looked around and took note that the showroom was clean, modern, well lit, and quite cosmopolitan with perhaps a slight bohemian twist. The back of the house, however, was what the young man's mother would have called "controlled chaos." She used that term whenever the young man or his siblings did not clean their room to the standard she was happy with. The young man said to Shelly, "What am I looking for?"

She responded, "Everything—the believability of it all. People who knew me growing up knew I was somewhat 'out there' and expected me to have a rather out there existence. I came from nothing! Both of my parents were working class people who never earned more than twenty thousand dollars a year—combined! I was supposed to be an 'also ran.' You know, get up, go to work, come home, and do it all again the next day. But, I didn't believe that—I believed I could be more! You see, when it comes to goals, they have to be your own, otherwise they could be too hard or too easy! Mine were too easy. The judges and the juries who sentenced me to a life of abysmal mediocrity made my goals too easy! They thought I didn't have what it takes to do more and to be more."

"What did you say to them?"

With a sneer on her face, Shelly said, "I told them to shove their judgments and their opinions up where the sun doesn't shine! Nobody—and I mean *nobody*—will tell me what to believe in and what I can do or must do to become successful. It is my life and it is up to me to put forth the energy and initiative to do whatever I want to do and to become whatever I want to become! I can't tell you how many people I told to mind their own business—that they have no right trying to judge my future. I had these conversations (actually fights) with my parents, my friends, and other assorted busybodies with more opinion than hard work and results in their bag of tricks!

"My mom and dad wanted me to sew but to work for someone else because I would have an easy life since I was unable to or incapable of running my own business. I loved my parents but, as I mentioned before, they never earned more than twenty thousand dollars a year combined. What experience or expertise did they have to tell me I couldn't run a business? Did they fail or succeed in business and know what it takes or doesn't take to be a success? Did they know what skills I have or don't have to run a successful business? *No!*

"My dad and I had a huge fight when I said to him, 'Thanks for all the support, Dad. I know you have so much experience running a business that this is obviously an informed decision you are making."

"Dad said, 'I love you Shell, and I want what is right for you.'"

"I told him, 'If you want what is right for me, then let me figure that out for myself, Dad. That's what's right for me!'"

"My friends told me I was just too flighty—I should concentrate on the creativity part of work and not the business side since I wasn't built for accounting and reading insurance policies. And you know what? I hate accounting and I hate reading insurance policies, but it is part and parcel to what I love and am passionate about, so I learned to do both, and now I actually like them!

"Listen to me, young man. Make your goals believable and make them believable to you! No one else matters when it comes to your goals—not your parents, not your wife or your fiancée, not your friends, and not your boss or your employer!

"Listen to this: someone was telling everyone he couldn't believe that someone like me was going to open up a business! I may have been in his company an entire hour in my whole life. He was a person I barely knew and whom I can guarantee did not know me. There you have it—he was my judge, my jury, and my executioner all rolled up into someone who has an opinion based upon . . . based upon what? I don't know!"

"Did you ever approach him about what he said?"

"Did I ever approach him? You're damn right I approached him. There is a piece of his ass hanging in my living room! I told him that my being a success or a failure has nothing to do with his opinion and it is meaningless to me, so why not keep it to himself! And, I did this in front of his wife and his friends. I ended by telling him that he would be much better off worrying about himself and his goals than mine, I can take care of myself. I asked him if he could take care of his life and his goals. He was smirking at me, as if what I said was meaningless, but I could see by the look on his face and in his eyes that I was hitting home. He told me not to worry about his goals and his life because he had them under control. I told him, *'So do I!'* "

The young man, seeing the look of defiant triumph in Shelly's eyes, started to applaud and said, "Bravo, bravo!"

Shelly began to smile and told the young man, "I have customers who travel from Europe for my dresses. Super models want my dresses. I have fabric custom-woven for me and I get my thread from special silk mills! I am making great money and I work hard. Guess what? I love making dresses and designing fabric and I also love reading insurance policies and negotiating real estate deals. I love it all, and it is all very, very believable—*to me!*"

Looking at her watch, Shelly said, "12:30, I have to get back to work!"

The young man rose with a feeling of fascination and motivation. He noticed that there were several people at the door waiting to get in. One of the people waiting, he recognized. He knew she was a famous actress. Shelly, seeing the recognition in his eyes, said, "Hey, don't gawk! She is about to spend twelve grand on a dress!"

The young man nodded.

Shelly told him to go back upstairs and see Sid, "He is waiting for you!"

The young man nodded again and left.

On his way up the elevator to return to Sid's office, the young man wrote in his My-Tyme:

Goals need to be attainable—goals need

to be believable to you, the goal-setter!

With communication comes buy-in,

with buy-in, comes believability!

Chapter Ten

Sid, smiling, was waiting for the young man at the elevator. The young man thought, how do these people do this? Are they telepathic?

Sid asked, "Well, young man, what did you think of Shelly?"

"Unbelievable!"

"I'll take that to mean in a good way!"

"Please do; it was meant in a *very* good way!"

"Please," Sid said in a mild-mannered, almost subservient voice, as though he was a butler and the young man was his employer, "Come with me."

The young man was led toward an office somewhat smaller than Sid's but nicely appointed. It was obvious that there is a pecking order to this organization and that the office where this person worked was somewhat below the stature of Sid, but not just a broker, someone higher in the organization than that.

The gentleman in the office rose to meet the two men. He was as old as Sid, maybe older, but he had a spryness, a litheness that was absent in Sid. At the front door of the office Sid said, "This is Mitch. Mitch, this is the young man everyone is talking about."

"Hum," said Mitch, "well, there must be something to him, he survived Huffburg and Shelly in the same month!"

All three of them laughed.

Sid continued, "Mitch is Resident Manager here. Basically, he is the boss of this operation."

Stunned, the young man said, "Oh, I thought *you* were, Sid."

Sid clapped the young man on the shoulder and said, "Been there, did that, don't want to do it again!"

Laughing, Mitch said, "Me, too! I just didn't have the energy to change offices with this old codger! So I let Sid keep the bigger office! "

Again, all three men laughed.

Mitch said to the young man, "Come on in. May I get you something to drink?"

The young man said that water would be fine. Mitch, saying that he would be right back, turned and left the office. The young man noticed the richly appointed office and was most impressed by the voluminous number of sales and sales management awards Mitch had received throughout the decades. The office walls were literally covered with frames containing awards. A moment later, Mitch appeared with a bottle of spring water and handed it to the young man with a paper napkin wrapped around the bottle.

"Thank you," the young man said.

"You are quite welcome," Mitch responded.

"I couldn't help but noticing the number of sales awards you have received throughout the years."

Looking at the wall containing the most awards, Mitch, with a genuine sense of modesty, said, "Oh, those." While waving his hand toward the wall in an irreverent dismissal, he said, "I have a million more at home in my library. I just don't have enough room for them all!"

"Well, I guess you were definitely a successful broker."

"That I was, actually. Let's use present tense—I'm not dead yet—I am a successful broker. But it is not because of these awards, it is because of the people I have assisted throughout the years in making them wealthy and in the friendships I have developed. It's not about the money. Now, don't get me wrong, I am a capitalist—the money is grand, but what is the use of having the world at your feet if the inhabitants of the world hate you?"

"Hum, I guess not much."

"Yes, you are right, not much at all!"

The young man shifted in his chair, picked up his water bottle, and took a sip. He looked at Mitch and asked him directly, "Please, tell me, what is the secret of your success in sales, ahh, I guess in making money, and in making friends, too?"

"Hey," said Mitch, "one question at a time! I'm too old to remember more than one question!"

Both laughed. Both settled back in their chairs—Mitch ready to speak, and the young man ready to listen.

Mitch breathed a contemplative sigh and began, "Well, young man, we are here on this wonderful afternoon to discuss the 'R' in smart, correct?"

The young man nodded "correct" back to Mitch.

Mitch continued, "The 'R' stands for realistic—when setting goals, you need to make sure that they 'fit in' to all areas of your life, that you have no conflicting goals, and you set your goals in such a way that you maximize your chance of success and minimize your chances for failure. Remember, young man, there are a million ways to fail in any endeavor, but there is only one way to succeed. That one way is what we are looking for!"

"Interesting," the young man said in a reflective tone.

"You think so? You haven't heard anything yet! Let me continue. I'll start by telling you a little something about what I do for a living. Sid and I started working for this company more than fifty years ago. Actually, we started on the same day, in the same position—we were both mailroom clerks! We were fresh out of high school. We did pretty well in high school; both of us were near the top of our class. I think that's why we were hired. I can't tell you that for sure since the gentleman who hired us has long since breathed his last.

"We both worked hard, very hard. We never tried to play politics with each other. We both started night school at the university's extension program, as it was called at the time. Yes, we worked hard, and we studied hard. Both of us earned a BS in Finance and Economics and ended up with an MBA in Finance and Marketing. By the time we got our BS degrees, we were brokers and doing quite well for ourselves. By the time we got our MBAs we were managers and had a team of brokers under us.

"We were with the brokerage house about ten years by then. We both married the same year; actually, we married two lovely young ladies who happened to be first cousins! Their mothers were sisters! Fine ladies they were, too, so were their fathers. We had many, many a merry Christmas as a family. And many, many a fine cookout on the Fourth of July."

"While the both of us knew a lot about setting goals, we both feel that it was the setting of realistic goals for ourselves and our sales teams that gave us the greatest effect and was the key driver toward our level of success."

The young man asked Mitch, "I guess I understand 'realistic' as a word. I mean, I can define it for you, but I am not sure what you mean by it in the context of goal-setting."

Pursing his lips, obviously in raw thought, Mitch paused a moment, then continued, "You said that you can define realistic. Go ahead!"

Placed on the spot, the young man shifted with a bit of unease in his chair and said, "Well, it means that you need to, er, I guess realistic means that you might have to, well, in the context of goal-setting, it is . . . I guess I *know* what realistic means, but I can't *tell* you what it is."

Mitch, picking up on the accents on the young man's words 'know' and 'tell,' asked him, "Tell me, what did Shelly tell you the synonym for attainable was?"

With rapidity the young man, happy that he could provide an answer he was comfortable with as being correct, said, "Believable! Goals need to be believable to you, the goal-setter!"

Laughing and placing both hands in front of his chest in a forward/backward motion Mitch said, "Whoa there big fella. I know you know the answer, don't get so excited!"

With a level of embarrassment, the young man smiled a tiny, crooked grin, put his head on his chest, and timidly squeaked out, "Sorry."

Mitch immediately saw the young man was engaged in a playful role of self-admonishment and laughed heartily at this. He loved it when young people had a sense of humor.

Mitch went on, "So, what do you think is a synonym for realistic?"

After a moment of silence that was beginning to be awkward, Mitch said, "Truthful. You need to be truthful, and guess who you need to be truthful with?"

"Yourself?"

"Are you asking me or telling me? I asked a question, your answer came out as a question. Didn't you ever hear that it is rude to answer a question with a question?"

Now it was the young man's turn to sense the humorous prodding of Mitch. He said, "Yes, someone told me that yesterday. I think it was Mr. Huffburg. You somewhat remind me of him! Anyway, our goals need to be realistic—truthful to us!"

"Good," said Mitch, while laughing at the comparison of him with Huffburg. "Now think about that word 'truthful' and how it relates to realistic goals. You can't lie about your abilities and you can't kid yourself when it comes to your level of capacity. If you try to lie, you are truly only lying to yourself!

"Let me give you an example. A friend of mine, his first name is Joe, worked here some years ago. He was a good employee, but the brokerage business just wasn't for him. He is a very successful Real Estate agent now. I guess you could say that he likes physical assets like dirt and bricks and mortar more than financial assets like stocks and mutual funds.

"Anyway, we graduated high school together and this happened about thirty years after we graduated, so we were in our late forties at the time. Joe was an avid runner in high school. This was before running or jogging was in vogue. Basically, he was a cross country runner; it was nothing for him to run twenty-five or thirty miles at a clip.

"Well, needless to say, Joe was somewhat on the thin side. Actually, he was very thin. Now, don't get me wrong, he was very fit. He had small, tight muscles and was very strong. I remember a fight he got into with a big bully back in eleventh grade. Joe was six feet tall and weighed about 170 pounds, and the bully was about six feet, three inches tall and weighed about 220 pounds. The fight started in the hallway and ended in the lobby. The bully never knew what hit him. This tall stringbean packed a wallop! Anyway, the point is, Joe was strong and fit.

"But something happened after he graduated from high school. He got fat! Actually, he stopped running—he had no need to continue to run. He started to work full-time right after high school in his father's plumbing business. We had a few of the same classes together at night, and he eventually got his BS degree in Business Administration. But, he was married, and had a few kids early in his marriage. When his father passed on, he decided he no longer wanted to be a plumber and, with his degree in hand, he got a job with us as a broker. At the time, Joe was about 270 pounds!

"He was working in my team and I gave a talk about setting goals for success. Joe put it in his mind that he was going to set a goal to lose weight—about eighty pounds. He made a general announcement to our sales team and everyone applauded him on his focus and commitment. But here is how he went about it and why setting realistic goals are so very important. We work late here. The market doesn't open until nine-thirty, so a nine o'clock start time is really about as early as most employees come in, unless they are working on a special project such as selling to a group of clients who start their day very early.

"Joe got himself in the habit of waking about seven forty-five, showering, having a bite to eat, then coming to the office at nine. His wife took care of the kids in the morning so that Joe could sleep a little longer.

"After he set his goal, things changed for him, at least for a day or two! The day he started his goal, he didn't wake up at seven forty-five, he got up at five, and he dressed in gym clothes and went to the high school track and proceeded to run around the track twelve times. Twelve times! That's three miles from someone who is close to being obese by the weight of an average fourth-grader, and hasn't run in over a quarter of a century! I ask you, young man, is that realistic?"

"Ah, no, I guess not!"

"You guess not! I guarantee you, it is *not* realistic! It is not being truthful with yourself. There was no way he could perform at his current physical level. He could have done his family and himself a great disservice if something bad happened. Do you get my drift?"

"Sure, he could have tripped and broke his leg and been out of work for a long time or, worse yet, he could have had a heart attack and died!"

"Precisely! That is why goals need to be 'realistic,' and by now you know I mean 'truthful'—at least be truthful to yourself."

"So what happened to Joe?" The young man asked with a true, curious interest.

He ran for the first time on Saturday morning; I know that because we always have our meetings on Friday mornings. He came into work on Monday morning, limping and grumbling under his breath about all the pain he was in. When I asked him what was wrong, and he explained what he had done. I really yelled at him. Actually, I called him a damn fool. I was really excited and a few people heard me. Joe was embarrassed and he quit not long after that. I probably overreacted, but I just could not believe that an intelligent man with a wife and a family could act so irresponsibly and hide behind the notion that his boss told him to set goals for himself! He just wasn't truthful with himself. Actually, and more accurately, he let his ego get in the way of reality! 'Realistic' and 'reality.' Do you see the similarities?"

With a nod of understanding, the young man said, "Yes, I sure do!"

"And, if something bad had happened to him, I think I would have blamed myself for not explaining realistic goal setting better. That is why I overreacted! I only wanted the best for him, hell, for everyone I work I work with – just the best!!"

The young man, with rapped attention continued to nod.

Mitch smiled back with the knowledge that the young man understood. He was impressed with the ability the young man had to absorb concepts so quickly. He went over to his desk and scrawled three letters, C-E-O, on his note pad. It was a simple reminder to call the CEO to let him know how impressed he was with the CEO's choice of person to share this knowledge with.

Mitch went over to his desk and opened the top drawer. He pulled out a business card and handed it to the young man. The card was a crisp white, with black raised letter print. It read:

Susan von Hoff, PhD

Professor of Physics

After the young man read the name on the card, he looked up at Mitch with an excited expression. He said, "I—" but he was interrupted by Mitch who said, "Yes, yes, I know you know her; you had her for class a few years back. And she remembers you, too. Apparently you are one of the few non-physics majors who got an A from her for the calculus version of Principles of Physics!"

The young man smiled—beamed, in reality—feeling proud that such a distinguished educator, known the world over for her work, would remember him.

He placed the card in his My-Tyme, and followed Mitch's lead to the office door. Mitch put his left hand on the young man's shoulder, and extended his right hand, which was quickly clasped by the young man's right hand.

After a hearty shake, Mitch said, "She is expecting you in about an hour, and you have at least a half an hour's drive to the university. She is in her office this morning running the numbers for a paper she is presenting soon. Don't be late; she hates late!"

The young man remembered how angry she would get at students who would arrive to class late. She would ask them in class after they got settled in why she had more respect for them then they had for her. 'Promptness,' she would say, 'is not only a virtue, it flatters the other person.' She would go on to say that the other person feels important when his or her guest arrives on time! She would ask late-comers if they would like the person who is going to be giving them their final grade feel important. The answer was always a resounding yes, followed by promises of promptness in the future; followed by a smile on Dr Sue's face.

The young man got to his car, opened his My-Tyme, and wrote:

There are many ways to fail,
but only one way to succeed.

Setting realistic goals means
being truthful with yourself.

Chapter Eleven

Time Specific—
The Vacation Spot of the Century: Someday I'll—

Doctor Sue's office was exactly as the young man remembered it—books lay in stacks, askew on bookshelves, piles of papers, journals, and more books on every chair, all over her desk, and on most walkable parts of the floor. One notable pile started on the floor and traveled vertically to a height of seven feet. Between the formidable piles balancing precariously on her desk, a small slit appeared. In a room-size setting it would be like a small, narrow hallway surrounded by two extremely high walls.

From that narrow strip in the middle of the desk appeared the round face of Dr. Sue, peering out through her enormously large round spectacles. A slightly taller version of the famous Dr. Ruth, she hurriedly circumvented several piles of haphazardly placed papers, one of which she hit with her shoulder, causing it to wobble precariously. The young man smiled at the thought of one his favorite teachers being pinned to the floor with a stack of her own manuscripts. He thought of how a picture would look of that with the caption, 'Physics professor proves the law of gravity.' "

By the time he had exhausted that humorous thought she was around the stacks and peered up at the young man through her glasses sitting atop her four-foot, eleven-inch frame. With precision honed from years of mathematical discipline, she methodically raised her right hand in an extension of greeting and said, "Well, young man, it has been awhile. How have you been?"

The young man was getting ready to answer, but by the time he started talking, Dr. Sue was already walking back to her desk and looking for a place for the young man to sit. She found a stool no more than ten inches high, but with several feet of papers and journals on it. With careful handling, she picked up the pile and placed it upon the floor behind her chair and said to the young man, "Come, sit!"

The young man surmised that her question about how he was probably not meant to be answered. He answered anyway, "I'm fine."

Dr. Sue turned around and with a look of puzzlement said, "What?" It came out with her native accent at full throttle as "Vhat?" The young man said, "When I came in, you asked me how I was, I answered I was fine. How are you?"

"Oh, oh, good, very good, I am fine, too."

They spent a few minutes catching up and the young man was once again impressed with Dr. Sue's brilliance. It exuded from her. She would not be able to hide her formidable intelligence, even if she made a conscious decision to do so.

After some brief small talk, she asked the young man if he would like a drink of water, since that was all she kept in her office. He wondered where she could possibly put, or later find, a bottle of water. He thought that it would be wise not to pose that question out loud and gave her a polite no.

The young man remembered with fondness the way Dr. Sue started out each lecture. She would prop the glasses on the edge of her nose and say in her thick Austrian accent, "Vell, Vhat shall ve chat about today? Ahh, yes—" And then go into her lecture.

For her part, Dr. Sue was looking for a notebook on her desk. She found it, looked at the young man, propped her glasses on the edge of her nose, and said, "Vell, Vhat shall ve chat about today? Ahh, yes—" And, looking at her notebook said, "We are to here to discuss the first 'T' in smart, correct?"

"Yes." The young man responded with politeness.

"Tell me something, young man, what was my biggest pet peeve with most students?"

"Ha, that's easy—being late."

"Yes, you are correct. And why was that such an annoyance to me, do you know?"

"Well, you always said that it had to do with respect. One of the easiest ways that we can respect each other is by respecting each other's time."

"Ah, you remembered perfectly! Do you know why I consider time so valuable?"

"No, not really. I mean I know why I consider it valuable, but aside from the respect issue, I'm not sure why you do."

"It is because it is a nonrenewable resource. Once a moment is gone, it is gone forever. But, that notion of 'here now, then gone' can motivate us. We can use time to our advantage."

"I'm not sure that I understand. I mean, I follow you that time is what we can call somewhat of a sunk cost in business, but how can we use that to our advantage?"

"A good question, young man. We can use time to anchor a deadline for our goals. By that I mean you need to put a definite deadline on the completion of your goal. If you do that and have a plan for obtaining your goal, there is a much better chance you will achieve the result you are looking for. Do you know what we call a goal without a deadline or definite timeframe attached to it?"

"I'm not sure."

"It's called a dream! If you want to take a grand vacation, then set a goal without a deadline and you can go to, 'Someday I'll'—" Dr. Sue laughed at her joke and was obviously pleased with herself.

The young man also laughed, not sure if it was because of her joke, or because of her reaction to her joke. In either event, he felt good, and he truly believed that the information Dr. Sue was giving to him was valuable.

"Can you see, young man, how not putting a timeline on your goal can actually increase procrastination?"

"No, I am not sure I see how that can happen."

"Then let me explain that to you. After all, I am a teacher!" Dr. Sue's eyes were bright, energetic, and full of intelligence. She continued, "If you set a goal without a deadline, it is very easy to put off the necessary actions—the behavior changes—necessary to achieve the goal.

"For example, let's say you have decided to lose some weight, say, oh, twenty pounds. Now you set the goal and you know that you have to burn more calories, so you decide to join a gym and work out more, and reduce your caloric intake, so you decide to eat better. Now you don't have a deadline on your goal, but you are doing okay. You get to the gym four times a week, and you are watching what you eat.

"But several weeks into your goal, you are at a party and they are serving cheesy crab cakes—your favorite! Now, if you had a deadline on your goal, say you had three weeks left and you had four more pounds to go, you would generate the necessary motivation to avoid the temptation. But, since you don't have a deadline, you rationalize that you can have a few of your beloved cheesy crab cakes since you are doing so well on your diet and workout regime so far. And you can always get back on the wagon tomorrow. So, you eat one, then you eat another, and you rationalize a third. By then you rationalize, 'What the hell, I have fallen so far of the wagon now, I might as well eat my fill!' The next day, you might say to yourself, 'Well, I was so bad last night, I might as well have those blueberry crepes that I love so much, then get back on the wagon after breakfast,' and so on!

"Do you see how you are procrastinating on what is important to you and achieving your goals because the winds of temptation were blowing hard and you did not have the requisite psychological armor to buffet those temptations?"

"Yes, I see your point." The young man thought about summer vacations when he was in grade school. He remembered the last day of school when he would write down the names of the books he wanted to read during the summer and the activities he wanted to accomplish. But he had no time frame. He rationalized that he didn't need a time frame since he had all summer. He thought of how summer looked and how summer felt when he was nine years old. Its span had such breadth and depth that it appeared to be seemingly endless. He figured that there was enough time to get everything accomplished. But, because he had no deadline for achieving his goals, he accomplished only a fraction of what he anticipated. The reason? Baseball, hide and seek, bike-riding, swimming, family vacation, and so on. All of the other fun activities nudged out the higher payoff activities he wanted to accomplish.

The doctor continued, "When you do establish a goal and place a deadline on its attainment, it is as if something magical happens. All of the necessary resources come into alignment and it is as if the universe comes to your aid to assist you in the accomplishment of your goals.

"Now, young man, I am a scientist! I know that nothing magical happens—it is all very scientific. You see, when you have a firmly established goal in your mind, and, of course, have it written down so that you may review it daily and make modifications when necessary, and have a firm deadline, your subconscious mind actually begins to make micro adjustments to your behavior, that assist you in attaining your goal in the time frame you have previously established. Thus, when they bring a tray of cheesy crab cakes past you and you have a deadline, you can say to yourself, 'I only have three weeks to go. So many people tonight have complimented me on how good I look, I only have four pounds to go and I remember I have three weeks to do it! I can do it! I don't need those damn, little fat balls!' And you say to the server, 'Ah, no thank you; I'm on a diet.' Whew! You did it! The temptation came, and went, and you survived because you had a firmly established goal and a deadline for its attainment. In other words, the mental scale that exists inside of you, and every one for that matter, is one side of the scale was the snack that would sabotage your diet and the other side was your self-image of being thinner, with a time-specific goal. The self-image side was heavier. Without the time frame, the self-indulgence side was heaver, and so was your backside the next morning!

"What do you think, young man? Does this process of setting timely goals make sense to you?"

With a note of excited enlightenment in his voice, the young man replied, "Oh yes, yes, it certainly does. If you set a goal without a deadline, it is almost useless."

"Yes," said the doctor, "And, not only useless, it might actually be deleterious to the achievement of the goal because it is allowing you to rationalize a level of procrastination. That procrastination can lead you to a very bad habit of repeating that process with other goals! Be careful with your thoughts and your action in terms of planning and achieving what you want out of life.

"Life is tricky. It actually never fails you; it gives you *exactly* what you ask for, but you had not only better ask for the correct thing, you'd also better ask for that thing correctly. If you say it wrong, you may not be happy with the results! If you constantly set goals and not hit them, and rationalize the missing parts of those goals—for example 'circumstances beyond your control'—you are setting yourself up for future failure based upon past performance! So, as I mentioned prior, be careful!"

The young man was blown away by Dr. Sue's comments, but more so by her obvious passion for goals and the timeliness necessary to achieve them. Sensing a dismissal was forthcoming; the young man rose, but did so in unison with the doctor. She laughed while saying to him, "I guess we are tuned into each other."

Laughing back the young man said, "Yes, I guess we are! Thanks you so very much, Dr. Sue. Your information was extremely valuable to me!"

"Actually young man, I think that it is valuable for everybody. You, however, have decided to listen!" Dr. Sue walked around her desk and returned to where she was sitting. She began to look around the top of the paper-strewn counter while asking herself, "Now, where is that card?"

Then, with a burst of enlightenment showing on her face, she said, "Ah, yes, here vee go!," and walked over to the young man again. I hope you are hungry; you need to be at this person's place of business at four. No later! He will probably only have half an hour to speak with you, so be sharp! Sunday is a very busy evening for him." Dr. Sue was smiling and so was the young man. They shook hands.

Then Dr. Sue did something extremely uncharacteristic for her, she grabbed the young man and gave him a very strong hug. As he left her office she said, "Be aware, young man. Always be aware. Life rewards those who pay attention! What will you do with the time that is given to you?" And with those parting words, Dr. Sue reentered her world of academic chaos.

The young man had about ninety minutes and was planning on stopping for a quick bite to eat. He was also puzzled about Dr. Sue's comment about being hungry until he looked at the business card he was handed. He then thought he needed to do something else for the next hour and a half besides eat. The card read:

Bella's Bistro

Gene Bella

Culinary Stud!!!

As he retired from Dr. Sue's organized chaos and headed toward his car, the young man assumed he was going to get a meal from Gene. He knew that he had some time to kill so he went to a local restaurant, ordered an ice tea, and began to write in his My-Tyme:

You need to put a definite deadline

on the completion of your goal.

A goal without a deadline is a dream.

A goal without a deadline can actually

cause you to procrastinate more.

Life rewards those who pay attention!

What will you do with the time

that is given to you?

He was beginning to get a feel for what success was all about. He was also getting a feel for goal-setting. As he continued to cogitate, he started to understand the relationship between success and goal-setting. It was if they were two sides of the same coin—As if you couldn't talk about one without talking about the other. The young man was excited. He loved the journey he was on!

Chapter Twelve

The young man arrived at the restaurant around 3:30. He knew he was early but promptness was one of his virtues. Even as a child, the young man was always early. He spent many a Saturday morning with his grandfather who would say, "I'll pick you up at six in the morning to go fishing," and he would be there at five-thirty. Many conversations occurred between "Pop-Pop" and the young man.

Pop-Pop was a businessman and owned a few small businesses during his working life. He never made a huge sum of money but, then again, money was not his primary goal. The young man's father, Pop-Pop's son, was one of seven children, actually eight, but one died several days after birth. Pop-Pop loved life, his family, and his faith. He was a cradle Catholic; he attended Mass and received Holy Communion daily. The young man discovered that the reason Pop-Pop showed up early for the fishing trips was because he attended 5:00 AM Mass and then came right over to the young man's house.

One thing Pop-Pop told the young man that he remembered through the years was that self-discipline is the precursor of personal freedom. The young man really didn't understand the concept, so Pop-Pop explained.

"You see, Lil Guy" (Pop-Pop's name for the young man. He had told the young man's father that if he has a nickname, then he can give a nickname!) "Self-discipline means that we can accomplish what we *need* to do so that we can then spend the rest of our time doing what we *want* to! If you think about it, we all have a morning routine—what we do when we wake up. You brush your teeth, eat breakfast, shower, and so on. Why not add to that list? For instance, plan your day—do some exercises, read, write, go to church. Get that stuff done, the stuff that if you don't do, you will feel guilty. Then you can go to work with a clear head, come home, and spend some time with your family. Then, when everything is calmed down, you will find that you have several hours to do whatever it is that you want to. Maybe it's watching television. Maybe it's meeting a few of your friends to shoot the bull. Maybe it's to sit with the love of your life and watch the sun set, or the moon rise. The point is that whatever you decide to do, you can do with a clear head and a light heart. Why? Because you did everything you had to, and now you can do what you want to!"

Pop-Pop died in his sleep, it was a shock to the family even though he was in his early eighties. The reason it was a shock to the family was because Pop-Pop was in such fabulous physical health and spirits.

The young man remembered talking to Pop-Pop about his child who had died a few days after birth, and Pop-Pop's eyes actually began to well up with tears. He told the young man, "That poor baby never knew riding a bike, or kissing a girl, or catching a football! He never had the chance. But, God knows better than I—if He calls, you go. Someday, we will all go. But, remember, Lil Guy, when a loved one is being lowered into the ground, a piece of you goes down there with that person!" And that is exactly how the young man felt when his Pop-Pop died.

While pondering in fond remembrance of what he learned from his grandfather, the young man was startled into current reality by several light thumps on the driver's side window. There, smiling at him, was a mid-to-late-thirties gentleman who could have been the picture on a poster titled, Italian Chef.

"Hey, I thought you were dead in there! My name is Gene, You want to come in, or just sit out here in your car?"

The young man said, "Oh! Sorry. Yes, I'll come in."

Gene was a tall, slender man with a thick crop of jet black hair and deep, dark olive eyes with subtle specks of brown dispersed through his irises. He walked with a somewhat self-confident shuffle that projected a cocky, not-a-care-in-the-world attitude that was exotic, almost charming. The crooked smile that turned up the right side of his mouth slightly was set there seemingly in perpetuity. The young man liked Gene immediately. As a child, Gene was probably the kid everyone wanted to hang around and wanted to be like.

The two men walked into the reception area of the restaurant that housed a coat room on the right and a podium atop which sat a ledger book with the night's reservations. To the left were a modest bar and eight leather-adorned bar stools. The restaurant had eight beers on tap and a shelf housed several dozen bottles of other beer available. The liquor selection was expansive and deep—many types of alcohol had several brands to choose from. The décor was classical Italian. The colors were muted and tasteful. The overall ambiance was that of subtle refinement and tasteful appointments.

There were no pointed fingers or red, white, and green posters with off color sayings, neither were there any parallels to the old mafia movies. There was no doubt that the facility was Italian and it served Italian food, but you couldn't quite put your finger on why it was Italian—it was that subtle. If the menu paralleled the décor, the young man was sure that most clients of the establishment left full, satisfied, and feeling as though the night and the investment in their meal was very well spent.

They walked toward the back of the establishment and into the kitchen. Half a dozen kitchen staff were busily preparing the night's fare. Huge trays of chicken were being par-baked, as well as other

127

main courses. The aromas wafting through the air were nothing less than dizzying. The young man's appetite was immediately whetted.

Gene, spending years noticing people's hungry looks, was instantly aware of his guests' needs. He walked the young man through the kitchen to a door in the very back of the building. Before opening the door, Gene turned around and said, "Gino, vieni qui." The young man understood that this must have meant for Gino to come over because a young man in his mid-twenties with brown hair in long loose curls came over. Gene said something in Italian to him. Gino responded in Italian. Then, both Gino and Gene looked at the young man for a moment and laughed, and then Gino hurried away.

The young man felt a bit uncomfortable but didn't say anything, though he felt that he may have been the brunt of a joke, albeit a good-natured joke. Gene entered into what was his personal office. It was not a large office, at least by comparison to the CEO's, but it was comfortable. It was nicely decorated and cluttered enough to let the young man know that this office was used more than just superficially—there was work done in here!

In front of a desk, the design was strikingly contemporary Italian. There were two leather, mated chairs that were taken from the dining area. Gene gestured for the young man to sit in one and Gene sat in the other. After a moment of mutual appraisal, Gene started, "Well, I guess we are here to discuss the final letter in SMART(T), correct?"

"Ah, yes, the second 'T' in smart."

Just then a knock sounded on the door and Gino came in carrying a covered tray and a small wooden stand. With lightning speed and precision, Gene's young assistant put the stand down, opened its closed legs, placed the tray atop the stand, removed the bright, silver cover, and waited for further instructions.

Sitting on top of the tray were several plates filled with various types of food. Each plate contained a portion of several different types of pasta. One was penne in a deep, rich, red vodka sauce. There was a pasta shell stuffed to the point of overage with both meat and cheese. Also, there was a small sample of a fra diavolo sauce over some linguine. In the center of the plate was a piece of grilled sausage, a rosemary spiced chicken leg, a small rolled steak stuffed with breadcrumbs and cheese, and a small piece of meat he found out later was rabbit in a delicate brown sauce.

On the side of each plate was a small Caesar salad. On top sat some shaved parmesan, several homemade croutons, and an anchovy.

Gene looked at Gino and said to him, "Gino, this food looks amazing. At it smells better than it looks, I can't wait to taste it . . ."

There was a moment of silence that led into another moment of awkward silence. Gino, asked, "Would you like me to leave the two of you?" Gene replied again that he would love to taste the food! Uncomprehending, Gino said, "Well, go ahead and eat."

"Shall I use my fingers," Gene asked, "or just stick my head in the plate?"

Gino slapped his forehead and said, "Sorry boss, be right back!" He returned in what seemed like an inordinately short time frame with two separately rolled napkins containing flatware, and said that he was sorry once again. Gene said that it was no problem and Gino left.

The young man witnessed this slight comedy but with a feeling of being disconnected—he was focused on the lovely plate of food that was before him. The look and smell were enough to get his appetite at full attention.

"Dig in," Gene said to him. "We'll talk in a few minutes."

Gino reentered the office with a basket of freshly baked garlic and herb bread, left it on the tray where the plates were, and left. His inconspicuousness and agility impressed the young man. What impressed him even more was the aroma wafting from the bread basket.

Several minutes turned into twenty minutes. Both men didn't talk much—they ate. Finally, Gene said, "My grandfather used to say to me in Italian, 'When you eat, you don't age.' " He patted his stomach. The young man noticed Gene's clean plate and realized that he was not far behind him. Gene smiled and said to the young man," Don't age? If you eat any more, I think you're gonna get younger!" The young man laughed and patted his stomach.

After a belch, which was close to being loud to the point of embarrassment, Gene smiled at the young man and said, "Okay, so what brings you here?"

The young man responded, "Uh, Dr. Sue!"

Gene smiled at the subtlety of the young man's humor and said, "Yeah, she's a fine lady. She and her husband are regulars here; at least twice, sometimes more per week."

"I guess we are here to talk about the last "T" in SMART."

"Ah, yes, my favorite part of goal-setting. Tell me, do you know what that "T" stands for?"

"Ah, no, not really."

"It stands for tangible. Well, now you know. So, tell me, what does tangible mean?"

After a moment of silent contemplation, the young man said, "I guess it means that you can touch it, right?"

"Not quite, at least not totally. Tangible means that it can be sensed. Touch is only one of the five senses. Look at it this way: Your mind is like a computer. It is a great processor, fast, efficient, always willing to do more. But, what does a computer need to give you good output?"

"Good input!"

"Right! And that comes from your senses! All five of them! The more senses you get involved with something, the greater the output, the richer it becomes. Let me ask you a question: why would you come here for an evening?"

"To eat."

"Oh, really? Come with me, young man."

Both men stepped into the kitchen where the dizzying aromas of the night's fare were still being skillfully prepared. They walked through the kitchen into the main dining area where the waitresses were sampling some of the food and talking among themselves about the best way to sell the items. When they got to the front of the establishment, Gene opened the door and both men walked outside. Gene turned around and faced the building, raised his arms and hands to his side in the shape of a Y, and asked the young man, "What do you see?"

"I'm not sure what you want me to say. I see the front of your restaurant."

"Keep going." Gene said this in a rather pointed way, so much, in fact, that the young man felt on edge to answer properly.

"Well, I see a building painted white. I see shrubs that are neatly trimmed and a clean parking lot. I see a set of really well-made, expensive-looking doors."

"Good." Opening the door and walking inside, Gene continued, "Now, tell me what you are experiencing. Bring the use of all your senses to bear and tell me what you are sensing."

The young man thought for a moment and said, "I smell some great food cooking. It's getting me hungry again, just smelling it. I see a well-furnished place that looks like it belongs in an Italian still life."

"Keep going. Use your other senses."

"Well, I hear the hustle and bustle of the kitchen employees, but in the background I hear some modern Italian music being played." The young man, understanding Gene's questions, went to the wall and felt it. He said, "I feel some great texture here, really expensive wall coverings." The young man walked over to a table and sat down. He said, "I feel the luxury built into this chair and the fine feel of the tablecloth. I felt the delicate texture of the food I ate—the snappiness of the pasta and the smooth texture of the rabbit. And I tasted the most marvelous food ever." Getting excited about his discovery, the young man continued, "I used all of my senses! Not just taste, but all of them! Ha, this isn't just a restaurant, it is an experience!"

Issuing a very broad smile, Gene said, "Yes, exactly! You hit the nail on the head. Look, I put out a great product. I suffer for my food. But people keep coming back because of the experience, not just the food, but everything combined—the entire sensory experience. That is why you have to make your goals tangible. You need to get as many of your senses involved in the process as you can!"

The young man's smile, turned down a little, then became a frown and he asked Gene, 'But, how? How do you make goals tangible?"

Still smiling, Gene said, "That's easy! What do you do if you want to buy a car?"

"Well, I would research which car to buy and then—"

Interrupting the young man, Gene said, "No, after that. You know which car you want. Now what?"

"Well, I need to pick the interior and exterior color, then—"

"Stop! Why wouldn't you do all of this research *before* you need a car, then determine which color you want and put a picture of that where you can see it often? Why wouldn't you visit car lots and take pictures of the *exact* car you want, even before you can afford to buy it? Why wouldn't you want to test drive it, just to get a feel for it? Why wouldn't you want to live that vehicle, tangibly? Why wouldn't you want to set a goal to buy the exact car you want, then surround yourself with information about that car with as many sensory impressions as you can? Then, when you finally get the vehicle of your dreams, it is almost like a déjà vu experience?

"Well, I guess I never thought of it that way."

"You should! When you set a goal, you have got to make it tangible. You need to get as many senses involved as possible. Those sensory impressions are what will drive your decisions and behaviors to accomplish your goals."

The young man was nodding his head, but, he was also shaking. Gene asked him if he was all right and the young man said that he was fine. But he felt as if he has reached the limit of his ability to comprehend.

Gene laughed and said, "Oh, information overload, huh?"

The young man said in a low, almost imperceptible voice, "Yes, I guess so. There is so much information here and the information is so exciting that I need to process it all. It is quite overwhelming!"

"I know just how you feel," Gene said as he clasped the young man on his shoulder while moving him slightly toward the front door. Gene continued, "You have a great deal of information to chew on. I would suggest that you talk to the CEO about everything you have learned during the past two days."

"Yes, I will see if I can get in to see him on Monday."

"Actually, if you don't leave soon, you will see him tonight. He has an early reservation with his wife this evening before they go to the concert. It would probably be better if you didn't see him here, it might be awkward."

"Oh, sure, I understand, I'll leave now. But by the way, what concert is he going to see, the Philharmonic?"

"Ha, you don't know your CEO very well, do you? He's going to see the Blue Oyster Cult. He has been following them for forty years. He met his wife at a BOC concert when they were in college! Don't get me wrong, he loves all types of music, but give him some classic rock or some '80's hair metal and he is one cool rockin' dude!"

Amazed, the young man said, "I have one more question for you."

"Shoot!"

"When you were talking to Gino in Italian, I felt that the two of you were making fun of me."

"We were!"

"Oh."

"I told Gino to get some food, because it looked like you were going to fall over from hunger. Gino said, 'Hey boss, if he goes down, I'm gonna put him in the soup!'"

Both men laughed.

Gene put on a serious face and told the young man, "Be at the CEO's home tomorrow morning at ten. No earlier, remember that he is going to a concert tonight!"

"His *home?*"

"Don't worry about that. Just be there; he will be. Gotta run, brother, I have people to feed. You know where he lives, right?"

The young man said, "Yes, I know, and thank you."

"No problem and it was my pleasure. Hey, keep eating; get some meat on those bones!"

Both men laughed and parted ways.

The young man got into his car, opened his My-Tyme and wrote:

Goals need to be tangible.

The more senses you get

involved setting a goal,

the more real it will become.

Get all five senses involved in

the goal-setting process.

I really like rabbit!!!

Epilogue

The End is the Beginning—Back to the CEO

The young man was at the CEO's home at 9:45. By 9:50 he was at the CEO's door and rang the bell. He noticed that the CEO's front door was ajar and the lights were on. Emerging from the bowels of the home a moment later was the CEO, decked out in a clean, neatly pressed pair of Levi Jeans and a black tee shirt that read, Blue Oyster Cult, On Tour Forever.

The huge, inviting, gracious smile beaming from the CEO's face was evident. He said to the young man, "Come in, please."

The CEO waited in the doorway and when the young man passed him, the CEO patted him on the shoulder, still smiling. The CEO said, "I would give you a tour of the house, but we need to make this quick." He took the young man into the library off of the foyer and both men sat in a reading area. Crossing his legs in an informal, yet unfamiliar way, the CEO, placed both clasped hands on his lap, and sat smiling and silent. The silence seemed to take on an awkward ambiance.

To break it the young man said, "Well, I guess you want to know everything I learned?"

The CEO laughed and said, "Young man, I already know everything you learned during the last two days! I taught it to most of the people you spoke with. I am more interested in what you are going to do with that information, how you plan to improve yourself with it, and how you plan to make more money for the corporation because of it."

The young man sat quietly for a moment. He was thrown off. He fully expected the CEO to ask him what he had learned, not how to apply it. How was he to answer? He was still digesting the information. It wasn't fully metabolized yet. This seemed to the young man to be an unfair question, and was about to tell the CEO that in a more politically correct way. But, the CEO was aware of the young man's thoughts and asked him, "Am I being too pointed with you? Are you not sure what to say, or how to respond?"

The young man noticed that the CEO was still smiling with that broad grin. Could it be, the young man thought, that the CEO was bantering with him? Perhaps, playing with him? Maybe trying to get him to think deeper? The young man relaxed a bit, took a deep breath and said to the CEO, "Well, I would have bet that you wanted to know everything I learned. I spent all of last night rewriting my notes, putting the material in order, practicing what I was going to say to you, and how I was going to say it! You really threw me off!"

"Ha," said the CEO. "That's my job, young man—to get people to think past the boundaries of their current existence and mind frame. How do you think this company hit the Fortune 100? Do you think it was my executives and me sitting around saying, 'Hey, let's do today what we did yesterday and hope for the best?' I can assure you that it was not! We need to be a better company today than we were yesterday. To do that we need to become better people, smarter people than we were yesterday. A great company has great people working for it. A smart company has smart people working for it. A world class company has world class people working for it! And, my job is to reinvent the people so that *they* can reinvent the company. I get them to reinvent their people so that they can reinvent their people and so on! But who reinvents me?

The young man said, "I don't know!"

The CEO said, "I do! I reinvent myself! I constantly set goals—new goals, exciting goals for myself. I figure out and plan how to attain them, and then I put that plan into action and I hit them! And guess what model I use?"

"The SMART(T) model?"

"And what else would I use? You have learned a great deal during the past two days; you learned how to define success and you learned how to set goals. Now, you need to get out there and set them. Then you need to plan how you are going to achieve them. Then you need to modify your behavior and act in such a way as to achieve them.

"Goal-setting is really a tool for behavior modification. The more you want, the more goals you set. The more goals you set, the more you need to change your behavior to achieve those goals. Get it?"

"Got it!"

"Good. Now, if you don't mind, young man. My wife is at the pool having a cup of coffee waiting for me. We need to leave very soon. We are going to have an early lunch with the band we saw last night, and then I need to catch a flight to China. Do you have any final questions for me?"

"Yes, well, I am still not sure on how to actually *set* goals. I understand the theory, but how do I really *do* it?"

"Practice."

"Is that it?"

Looking at his watch and sounding slightly frustrated the CEO asked, "Young man, how do you get good at playing the piano?"

"You practice."

"Correct. In other words, you play the piano. And, how do you get good at golf?"

"You play golf."

"Ah, you are beginning to understand. And how do you get good at setting goals, modifying your behavior, and achieving your goals?"

"I guess by setting goals."

"Yes, yes. You need to set goals and work with the process you have just learned. Have fun, it should be an enjoyable process. You will make mistakes, just as practicing the piano or golf, but mistakes are part of the growth process."

The young man said, "I understand what you are saying, but I am still confused on the nuts and bolts of what to do—the actual way that you work out the plan."

With a smile on his face, the CEO stood up, as did the young man. He walked the young man to the door of his home, and said, "Young man, we will talk again. What you are asking me is a whole other discussion. Play with this process for a while."

"How long?"

"A few months, maybe a year, then come back to see me."

"A *year?* Will you give me the answers I am asking you for then?"

"No! But, by then you will have a deeper understanding of the goal-setting process so that I can give you a better quality question for you to answer yourself!"

"So, it's up to me to work out the rest of the goal-setting process?"

"Well, maybe in the short run, but I'll be around to help. Much of what you are asking is a whole other discussion. Young man, you are on a very exciting journey! Enjoy the ride!"

And with that statement, the CEO turned, and went back into his home.

The young man was not to see the CEO for six months. When they did meet again, it was at the CEO's house.

Look for the results of that meeting and the new journey of the young man in the second installment of *GoalsBook*, titled,

GoalsBook 2, The Field Book:

Putting Goal-setting to Work.

The young man went home that Monday evening feeling energized, excited, and full of passion yet also nervous, dismayed, and full of angst. Life yawned before him in its seemingly infinite expanse. What was he to do? What was he to focus on?

He thought he would begin by summarizing each of his appointments.

And the first part of his answer became very clear, he just needed to start. The CEO was correct—the young man was on an exciting journey!

Are you ready to begin yours?

The My-Tyme is a wonderful system for organizing your life. It evolved around the traditional features of a calendar and commitment system—time management—but it goes much, much further. The My-Tyme actually assists you in tracking your goals and arranging your goals into bite-sized nuggets that can be accomplished on a daily basis.

You can find information about the My-Tyme on my Web site:

Intelligentmotivationinc.com

Or you can call My-Tyme directly at:

800 – 876 – 2389

Make sure when you call that you tell the customer service representative you are calling as a result of *GoalsBook*, thereby guaranteeing the best price possible.

CPSIA information can be obtained at www.ICGtesting.com
Printed in the USA
BVOW031943070113

310013BV00001B/1/P

9 780985 394929